Vanessa's Miracle, A Journey Through Kidney Cancer

Amanda Ventura

Published by Amanda Ventura, 2024.

VANESSA'S MIRACLE, A JOURNEY THROUGH KIDNEY CANCER

First edition. September 28, 2024.

ISBN: 979-8224780341

Written by Amanda Ventura.

Table of Contents

VANESSA'S MIRACLE
A Journey Through Kidney Cancer

ACKNOWLEDGEMENT

In the journey of writing this book, I have often found myself reflecting on the profound challenges faced by those battling cancer and other life-altering circumstances. To all the readers who find themselves navigating these difficult paths, I want to extend my deepest gratitude and admiration. Your strength, resilience, and unwavering spirit inspire me every day.

This book is dedicated to you, the fighters, the survivors, and the caregivers. Your stories of courage illuminate the darkest moments and remind us all of the power of hope and community. Thank you for sharing your journeys, for teaching us about vulnerability and perseverance, and for showing us that even in the face of adversity, we can find moments of joy, connection, and understanding.

I am honored to walk alongside you through these pages, and I hope that my words provide comfort, insight, or perhaps a spark of inspiration in your own battles. May you continue to find strength in your stories and support in each other as you navigate the road ahead.

With heartfelt appreciation,

Amanda Ventura

DEDICATION

To my mother,

This book is dedicated to you, a true warrior in every sense. Your battle against kidney cancer has been a testament to your remarkable determination, strength, and resilience. I am endlessly inspired by the way you face each obstacle and challenge head-on, exhibiting a courage that leaves me in awe.

Your unwavering dedication to keep fighting and your refusal to give up are qualities that light the way for all of us. Thank you for teaching me the true meaning of perseverance. I love you more than words can express, and I am so proud to be your daughter.

With all my heart,
Amanda Ventura

Introduction

In the quiet moments of life, when the world seems to stand still, we often find ourselves reflecting on the battles we face and the strength we possess. Vanessa's story is one of those remarkable journeys that defy the ordinary. Diagnosed with stage Four kidney cancer at a time when she was embracing the vibrancy of life, Vanessa was thrust into a fight that would test her resilience, challenge her spirit, and ultimately reveal the depths of her courage.

This book chronicles Vanessa's extraordinary journey-a path filled with uncertainty, fear, and heartache, but also one illuminated by hope, love, and the unwavering support of family and friends. From her initial diagnosis to the grueling treatments and the moments of despair, Vanessa's experience resonates with anyone who has faced adversity. Yet, it is also a story of miracles-of small victories that paved the way for a larger triumph.

Through her struggles, Vanessa discovered not only her own strength but also the profound connections that bind us all in times of crisis. Her journey is a testament to the power of the human spirit, the importance of community, and the belief that even in the darkest moments, there is a light to guide us forward.

Join us as we delve into Vanessa's battle against kidney cancer-a tale of resilience, hope, and the miraculous strength that lies within us all. This is not just a story of survival; it is a celebration of life, love, and the unbreakable spirit of a woman who refused to be defined by her illness.

Chapter One

The Calm Before the Storm

In the small town where Vanessa lived, life had a comforting rhythm. The mornings began with the aroma of freshly brewed coffee wafting through her kitchen, and the days were filled with laughter shared among friends and family. Vanessa, a vibrant woman, was known for her infectious spirit and unwavering optimism. She was the type of person who could light up a room with her smile and whose laughter could chase away the clouds of any gloomy day. Yet, as the seasons changed, a silent storm was brewing beneath the surface, one that would test her resilience like never before.

It all began with subtle signs, a slight discomfort in her side that she attributed to stress from work. Life was demanding, and Vanessa often pushed herself to meet deadlines and exceed expectations. She was used to ignoring minor aches and pains, chalking them up to the everyday wear and tear of a busy life. But as weeks passed, the discomfort morphed into a persistent nagging sensation that refused to fade away, prompting her to schedule an appointment with her doctor.

The day of her appointment arrived, and Vanessa felt a mix of anxiety and determination. Sitting in the sterile examination room, she glanced at the medical posters adorning the walls, each one depicting a happy, healthy body. Little did she know that her own body was harboring an unwelcome intruder. As the doctor entered, his demeanor was calm but serious, and Vanessa sensed that this was a pivotal moment in her life. The words "kidney cancer" echoed in her mind, shattering the illusion of normalcy she had clung to.

Vanessa's world tilted on its axis as she tried to process the gravity of the diagnosis. The doctor explained the next steps, but her thoughts were a whirlwind of emotions-fear, confusion, and disbelief. How could this be happening to her? She had always been the embodiment of health and vitality, and now she was faced with a battle that felt insurmountable. In that moment, the life she knew began to slip away, replaced by a harsh reality that she could scarcely comprehend.

After leaving the doctor's office, Vanessa sat in her car, staring blankly at the steering wheel. The vibrant colors of the world outside felt muted, overshadowed by the weight of her diagnosis. The familiar sound of birds chirping and children playing in the park nearby seemed distant and irrelevant. Tears streamed down her cheeks as the realization washed over her, this was the moment that would change everything. The calm she had known was gone, replaced by an impending storm that loomed on the horizon.

In the days that followed, Vanessa grappled with her new reality. She spent hours researching kidney cancer, immersing herself in medical literature and personal stories from those who had walked a similar path. The information was both empowering and overwhelming, offering a glimpse into the challenges she would face while also providing hope through stories of survival. Each night, as she lay in bed, her mind raced with questions and fears: What would treatment be like? Would she lose her hair? How would her loved ones cope with her illness?

Despite the uncertainty, Vanessa found solace in the support of her family and friends. They rallied around her, offering words of encouragement and unwavering love. Group texts filled with inspirational quotes and memes became a lifeline for her, a reminder that she was not alone in this fight. Yet, beneath the surface, Vanessa felt a sense of isolation; no one could truly understand the turmoil she was experiencing internally. The calm before the storm had been shattered, and she was left to navigate the turbulent waters of fear and anxiety on her own.

As the weeks unfolded, Vanessa began to prepare for the storm that lay ahead. She scheduled appointments with specialists, sought second opinions, and formulated a treatment plan that felt like an uncharted course. Each decision was heavy with significance, a testament to her determination to fight for her life. The calm moments became precious, as she soaked in the love of her family and cherished every spontaneous outing with friends. They took her to dinner, went for walks, and shared laughter that echoed like a soothing balm against the chaos brewing within her.

It was during one of these outings that Vanessa experienced a moment of clarity. Surrounded by loved ones, she realized that while the diagnosis was daunting, it did not define her. She was more than just a patient; she was a mother, a daughter, a friend, and a fierce warrior ready to confront the storm. With renewed resolve, she made a promise to herself. She would not let fear dictate her journey. Instead, she would embrace each day with gratitude and courage, finding joy in the little things, even amid the uncertainty.

As the day of her first treatment approached, Vanessa felt a mixture of dread and anticipation. The storm was no longer a distant threat; it was right at her doorstep. But in the face of the impending challenge, she discovered an unexpected wellspring of strength within herself. The fear that had initially consumed her began to morph into a sense of purpose. Each day leading up to her treatment, she focused on gathering tools to help her cope: creating a vision board filled with images of her goals, mantras of hope, and reminders of her loved ones who stood by her side. This tangible representation of her determination served as a beacon, guiding her through the uncertainty that lay ahead.

On the eve of her treatment, Vanessa gathered her closest friends and family for a small gathering at her home. They shared stories, laughter, and tears, creating a tapestry of memories that would sustain her through the challenges to come. She looked around the room, feeling the warmth of their presence envelop her like a comforting blanket. In that moment, she realized that she didn't have to face this battle alone; she had a strong support system ready to walk every step with her. This realization filled her with a sense of comfort, reminding her that love and connection could light even the darkest paths.

As dawn broke on the day of her first treatment, Vanessa felt the weight of the world on her shoulders, but she also felt an undeniable surge of hope. She donned her favorite outfit, a bright yellow dress that symbolized sunshine-a reminder of better days ahead. Looking in the mirror, she practiced her smile, determined to greet the day with positivity. She made her way to the treatment center, her heart racing as she entered the building, where the sterile smell of antiseptic mingled with the nervous energy of patients awaiting their sessions.

Sitting in the waiting area, Vanessa observed the other patients around her, each person with their own unique story and struggle. She felt a profound sense of camaraderie with them, even if they were strangers. The reality of their situations resonated with her, and she understood that they were all fighting their own battles against the storm. In that space, surrounded by others who shared her experience, she realized that vulnerability could also be a source of strength. It was okay to be scared, and it was okay to seek connection in the midst of uncertainty.

When her name was called, Vanessa took a deep breath and stood up, feeling the weight of the moment. As she walked down the long corridor, she could hear the beeping of machines and the soft murmurs of medical staff, a symphony of care that filled her with both anxiety and reassurance. She entered the treatment room, which was bright and filled with natural light. Nurses greeted her with warm smiles, and she felt a sense of calm wash over her as they prepared her for the procedure. They explained every step, reassuring her that she was in capable hands.

As the treatment began, Vanessa settled into the recliner, gripping the armrests as the IV needle was inserted into her arm. A rush of adrenaline coursed through her as the medication flowed into her veins. In that moment, she felt a mix of fear and empowerment, recognizing that she was actively fighting back against the disease that threatened her life. She closed her eyes and envisioned herself surrounded by a protective light, imagining each dose of medication as a powerful ally in her fight against cancer.

The minutes turned into hours, and Vanessa filled her time with music, podcasts, and text messages from friends sending her love. Each message was a reminder of the life waiting for her beyond the treatment room, a life filled with laughter, love, and countless adventures yet to come. She visualized herself healed, embracing the future with open arms. As the treatment session came to an end, she felt an unexpected sense of relief wash over her- a small victory had been achieved.

Walking out of the treatment center, Vanessa noticed the world outside was vibrant and alive. The sun shone brightly, casting golden rays that danced on the leaves of nearby trees. She took a moment to breathe deeply, feeling the fresh air fill her lungs. This was a new chapter, and although the storm was still raging, she had taken the first step on her journey. With her heart full of hope and determination, she knew she would face whatever came next with grace and courage, ready to embrace the challenges ahead and celebrate the miracles along the way.

Chapter Two

Signs and Symptoms

In the quiet moments before the storm of treatment began, Vanessa often reflected on the subtle signs that led to her diagnosis. Like many, she had brushed off her symptoms as mere inconveniences, attributing them to the stresses of daily life. But as she delved deeper into her experience, she came to understand that awareness of her body was the first step in identifying something truly alarming.

It all started with a persistent discomfort in her side. At first, it felt like a dull ache, easily ignored amid the hustle of her busy schedule. She often attributed it to her long hours at the office or the occasional late-night workout, rationalizing that her body was simply reacting to the demands she placed on it. But as the weeks turned into months, the discomfort evolved into something more pronounced-a nagging sensation that refused to dissipate, compelling her to take note of its presence.

Alongside the discomfort, Vanessa began to experience fluctuations in her energy levels. One moment, she would feel invigorated, ready to tackle the day, while the next, she would be drained and lethargic. It was a confusing juxtaposition that left her questioning whether she was simply overworked or if something more was at play. The fatigue was not just physical; it seeped into her mental state, causing her to feel foggy and unfocused, as if a cloud had settled over her thoughts.

Another alarming symptom emerged in the form of unexplained weight loss. As someone who had always maintained a healthy weight through a balanced diet and regular exercise, Vanessa was startled to find that her clothes were suddenly looser. The changes were gradual at first, but soon she could no longer dismiss them as a result of her busy lifestyle. Each time she stepped on the scale, the numbers seemed to mock her, whispering that something was wrong beneath the surface.

Accompanying the weight loss was a troubling change in her appetite. Foods that once excited her began to lose their appeal, and meals felt like more of a chore than a pleasure. She found herself skipping meals and ignoring her body's hunger cues, convinced that she simply didn't have time to eat amidst her hectic schedule. Deep down, however, she sensed that this aversion to food was a signal, an indication that her body was grappling with something beyond her control.

As if the physical symptoms weren't enough, Vanessa also experienced noticeable changes in her urination patterns. She found herself needing to go to the bathroom more frequently, yet felt an unsettling urgency that left her feeling uncomfortable. The strange combination of increased frequency and discomfort was puzzling, and she couldn't help but wonder if it was merely a result of increased water intake or something more significant. Nevertheless, she tucked this observation away in the back of her mind, convincing herself that she would address it when time permitted.

With each passing day, Vanessa's body felt like it was sending her mixed signals. She began to notice an unusual swelling in her abdomen, accompanied by a feeling of fullness that lingered despite not having eaten much. This sensation was disconcerting, and it made her acutely aware of how disconnected she had become from her own body. The reality was that she had been so focused on the external pressures of life that she had neglected to listen to the internal messages her body was sending her.

As Vanessa finally made the decision to seek medical advice, she felt a wave of relief mixed with trepidation. The act of reaching out for help was both empowering and terrifying. She knew that it was time to confront the nagging symptoms that had haunted her for months. Armed with a list of her concerns, she walked into the doctor's office, ready to uncover the truth about what was happening inside her.

The doctor listened intently as she recounted her symptoms, and Vanessa could see the shift in his expression as he began to connect the dots. Her descriptions of discomfort, fatigue, weight loss, appetite changes, and urination issues all pointed to a potential issue that required further investigation. He recommended a series of tests, including blood work and imaging scans, to determine the underlying cause of her symptoms. In that moment, she realized that the calm she had clung to was quickly evaporating, replaced by a sense of urgency.

As the tests were scheduled, Vanessa found herself grappling with a mix of hope and fear. She had taken the first step toward understanding her body, but the uncertainty of what lay ahead weighed heavily on her. It was a lesson in the importance of listening to her body, a realization that many often take for granted. The signs and symptoms she had initially dismissed were now stark reminders of the fragility of health and the necessity of vigilance in the face of adversity.

In the days leading up to her diagnosis, Vanessa felt a growing sense of clarity. The journey from denial to acceptance had been challenging, but it had also ignited a fire within her. She was determined to face whatever came next, armed with knowledge and a fierce resolve. As she waited for the test results, she immersed herself in research, seeking to understand kidney cancer and its implications. The more she learned, the more empowered she felt. Knowledge, she realized, could be a double-edged sword, but she was committed to wielding it in a way that would ultimately support her journey.

The waiting room became a paradoxical space for Vanessa. It was filled with anticipation yet heavy with uncertainty. Each tick of the clock felt like a reminder of the gravity of her situation. She watched as others came and went, some wearing expressions of relief while others harbored the weight of worry. In those moments, she silently prayed for strength,not just for herself, but for everyone navigating their own battles. The shared experience of vulnerability forged an unspoken bond among them, one that transcended the barriers of their individual stories.

When the fateful day arrived for her to receive the results, Vanessa entered the doctor's office with a mix of trepidation and determination. The walls felt like they were closing in, amplifying her anxiety. As she sat across from her doctor, she could see the seriousness in his eyes. He began to explain the findings, and Vanessa braced herself for the words that would change everything. The diagnosis of kidney cancer struck her like a bolt of lightning, electrifying her entire being. It was as if the ground had shifted beneath her feet, leaving her to grapple with a new reality.

As she processed the news, a wave of emotions washed over her, fear, anger, confusion, and a flicker of hope. The doctor explained the stage of her cancer and the options available for treatment. Vanessa listened intently, fighting to absorb the information while simultaneously wrestling with the emotions that threatened to overwhelm her. She understood that knowledge was power, but in that moment, it felt like a heavy burden. This was no longer just a series of symptoms; it was a life-altering diagnosis.

In the days following her diagnosis, Vanessa leaned heavily on her support network. Friends and family rallied around her, offering encouragement and love. Each phone call, text message, and visit served as a reminder that she was not alone in this fight. They became her lifeline, a source of strength that bolstered her resolve in the face of uncertainty. Together, they navigated the complexities of her treatment options, researching specialists and gathering information to create a plan that felt right for her.

With the support of her loved ones, Vanessa decided to take an active role in her treatment. She sought out second opinions, explored alternative therapies, and engaged in conversations with medical professionals who specialized in kidney cancer. The process was daunting, but it also ignited a newfound sense of purpose. Each piece of information she gathered became a tool in her arsenal, equipping her to combat the disease that threatened her life.

As she began treatment, Vanessa found solace in documenting her journey. She started a blog to share her experiences, not just to keep her loved ones informed but to connect with others facing similar battles. Writing became a cathartic outlet, allowing her to express her fears, hopes, and everything in between. It was a way to channel her emotions into something constructive, creating a space for dialogue and support while helping to raise awareness about kidney cancer.

In the midst of her journey, Vanessa also rediscovered the importance of self-care. She committed to practices that nurtured her body and spirit, experimenting with meditation, yoga, and creative outlets like painting and journaling. Each practice served as a reminder that amidst the chaos, she could cultivate moments of peace. These small acts of self-love became essential as she navigated the ups and downs of treatment, providing her with the resilience needed to confront the challenges ahead.

As the weeks turned into months, Vanessa found herself transforming in ways she never anticipated. The experience of facing cancer stripped away the superficial layers of her life, revealing a deeper understanding of what truly mattered. She learned to cherish the moments of joy, however small, and to embrace vulnerability as a source of strength. The storm she faced was daunting, but it was also a catalyst for growth, pushing her to redefine her priorities and values.

With every treatment session, Vanessa felt the weight of her diagnosis shift from a source of fear to a challenge she was determined to overcome. Each day brought its own set of trials, but she faced them with a newfound grit, fueled by the love of her friends and family. The journey was far from over, but she was no longer just a passive participant; she was an active warrior, ready to fight for her life and reclaim her future.

Ultimately, Vanessa's story was one of resilience and transformation. The signs and symptoms that had once signaled a dark chapter in her life became the catalysts for a profound journey of self-discovery and empowerment. As she continued down the path of treatment, she carried with her the lessons learned along the way-a powerful reminder that even in the face of adversity, the human spirit can rise and adapt. Each milestone in her journey, whether it was a small victory or a lesson learned through hardship, fortified her resolve. Vanessa understood now that she was not defined by her diagnosis, but rather by her response to it. With each passing day, she embraced the strength of community, the importance of self-care, and the unyielding belief that hope and healing could coexist, even in the darkest of times. As she stood on the precipice of her future, she was determined to share her story, inspire others, and remind everyone that life, with all its complexities, was a precious gift worth fighting for.

Chapter Three

The Next Doctor's Visit

Vanessa had been dreading her next doctor visit for weeks. The memories of the last appointment still lingered in her mind-the somber expressions of the medical team, the hushed conversations about her prognosis, and the daunting prospect of further treatments. However, this time felt different. She had been on Radvax therapy for a few months now, and while the side effects were challenging, she felt a flicker of hope igniting within her. Little did she know that this visit would be unlike any other.

As she entered the hospital, Vanessa took a deep breath, trying to calm the butterflies in her stomach. The familiar scent of antiseptic filled the air, and the fluorescent lights buzzed overhead-a stark reminder of her ongoing battle with cancer. Yet today, her heart raced not with fear, but with a sense of anticipation. The Radvax therapy had been described as groundbreaking, and she hoped it would bring the results she so desperately wanted.

The waiting room was filled with patients, each lost in their own thoughts and worries. Vanessa glanced around, noticing the weariness etched on their faces. She felt a sense of camaraderie with them, each person fighting their own battles. But today, she was determined to focus on her journey and the miracles that could happen in the world of modern medicine. With each passing minute, she wondered if the therapy had worked on the tumors that had spread to her brain.

When Vanessa was called in for her appointment, her heart raced with a mixture of excitement and anxiety. The doctor entered the room with a warm smile, and Vanessa felt a wave of relief wash over her. He reviewed her medical history and the progress she had made since starting Radvax. The initial scans had shown a grim picture, but her doctor was optimistic. As he prepared to share the results of her latest imaging, Vanessa's heart pounded in her chest.

"Vanessa," the doctor began, his voice steady yet filled with emotion, "I have some incredible news." Her breath caught in her throat as she leaned forward, eager for every word. "The tumors in your brain have remarkably disappeared. It's as if they were never there." For a moment, time seemed to stand still. The weight of his words settled in her mind, and disbelief and joy collided within her.

"Are you serious? Disappeared?" Vanessa could hardly contain her excitement, her eyes widening in astonishment. The doctor nodded, his expression a blend of professionalism and genuine happiness. He explained that Radvax therapy had demonstrated unprecedented results in certain patients, and Vanessa had become one of those extraordinary cases-a living testament to the power of medical innovation and human resilience.

Tears of gratitude streamed down her face as the reality of the news sank in. She had spent countless nights grappling with fear, wondering if she would ever see her children grow up or share precious moments with her loved ones. Now, it felt as if a heavy burden had been lifted from her shoulders. She was ready to embrace the future that lay ahead, filled with hope and renewed determination.

The doctor proceeded to discuss the next steps in her treatment, emphasizing the importance of ongoing monitoring and support. Vanessa felt a sense of empowerment as she listened, realizing that she had become an active participant in her healing journey. The Radvax therapy had not only addressed the physical aspect of her illness but also ignited a fire within her—a desire to advocate for herself and others facing similar challenges.

As she left the office, the world outside seemed brighter and more vibrant. The sun shone down on her, illuminating her path as if celebrating her victory. She couldn't wait to share the news with her family, to see the joy on their faces and the relief that would wash over them. The thought of reuniting with her children filled her heart with warmth, and she envisioned a future where they could create cherished memories together.

In the days that followed, Vanessa embraced this new chapter with open arms. She became an advocate for Radvax therapy, sharing her story and inspiring others in the cancer community. Her experience became a beacon of hope for those still fighting their battles, reminding them that miracles could happen, even in the darkest of times. Vanessa discovered strength she never knew she had, fueled by the love of her family and the knowledge that she was not alone in her journey.

As she reflected on her experience, Vanessa realized that the true miracle was not just the disappearance of her tumors but the transformation of her spirit. She had emerged from the shadows of despair, ready to embrace life with newfound gratitude. Each day became a gift, and she vowed to live it to the fullest, cherishing every moment and using her voice to uplift others along the way. In her heart, Vanessa knew that hope had the power to heal, and she was living proof of that truth.

As Vanessa settled into her new routine of rehabilitation, a profound sense of gratitude filled her heart. Each day began with a prayer, where she praised God not only for her miraculous healing but also for the strength that had allowed her to face the challenges ahead. She reflected on the journey of recovery from the damage caused by her illness and the treatments she had undergone. Each step, though daunting, was a testament to the divine support she felt enveloping her, urging her to push through the pain and uncertainty.

The journey to walk again was not easy. Vanessa had lost significant muscle strength during her treatment, and her body bore the marks of her struggle. Yet, in her heart, she felt a fire ignited by her faith. With each morning, as she prepared to face the daunting task of standing and taking those first tentative steps, she reminded herself that God was with her. She felt His presence in the quiet moments, whispering words of encouragement, reminding her that she was never alone in this journey.

With the support of her physical therapist, Vanessa embarked on her rehabilitation journey. The therapy sessions were filled with moments of frustration as she grappled with her weakened state. There were days when the effort felt insurmountable, and she questioned whether she would ever regain her strength. Yet, in those moments of doubt, she would close her eyes and pray, asking God for the perseverance to keep going. Miraculously, she often found that strength bubbling up from within, propelling her forward when she felt like giving up.

Vanessa set small, achievable goals for herself. Each day, she would aim to take just a few more steps than the day before. On some days, the progress felt minimal, but she learned to celebrate even the smallest victories. The first time she managed to walk across the room, tears of joy streamed down her face as she raised her hands in praise to God. It was a moment of triumph, a reminder that her body was healing, and that she was taking charge of her life once again.

As weeks turned into months, Vanessa's determination grew stronger. The physical therapy sessions became a sacred space where she would not only work on her body but also connect with God. Each time she struggled to lift her legs or balance herself, she would whisper prayers of gratitude for the strength He had bestowed upon her. The act of walking transformed into a spiritual journey, each step a testament to her faith and her commitment to reclaiming her life.

On particularly tough days, when the pain seemed unbearable, Vanessa would find solace in her faith. She reached out to friends and family, sharing her struggles and asking for prayers. Their unwavering support became a lifeline, reminding her that she was surrounded by love and encouragement. Vanessa often found herself leading prayer circles, where she would not only seek strength for herself but also uplift others facing their own battles. This shared faith reinforced her belief that God was working through her, providing the strength she needed to keep moving forward.

With each passing day, Vanessa's physical strength began to return, but it was the emotional and spiritual growth that truly amazed her. She realized that this journey to walk again was more than just a physical recovery; it was a profound transformation of her spirit. Her faith had deepened, and she recognized that the very act of reclaiming her ability to walk was a reflection of God's grace in her life. She felt called to share this message of hope with others who faced similar trials.

One day, while on a walk outside, Vanessa paused to take in the beauty of her surroundings. The sun was shining, the birds were singing, and she felt an overwhelming sense of peace. In that moment, she lifted her hands to the sky and praised God for the miracle of her healing and the strength to fight for her life. It was a moment of pure gratitude, where she acknowledged not just the physical aspects of her recovery but also the emotional and spiritual renewal she had experienced. She felt as if she were walking not only on the ground but also in grace.

As she continued to regain her strength, Vanessa started to explore new ways to express her gratitude. She participated in walks for cancer awareness, using her journey to inspire others. Each step she took in those events was a testament to her faith and resilience, and she wore a shirt that read, "Every Step is a Miracle." With each stride, she felt God's presence beside her, cheering her on and reminding her of the strength that had carried her through the darkest moments.

In the quiet moments of reflection, Vanessa acknowledged the power of her faith as a catalyst for healing. She praised God for every ounce of strength that had allowed her to rise from her bed and take those first steps. It was a reminder that, even in the face of adversity, faith could move mountains. Vanessa had learned that her journey was not just about her own healing but about inspiring others to find their strength in faith.

Vanessa sat in the waiting room, her heart racing as she clutched the edges of her chair. The sterile smell of antiseptic and the muted sounds of muffled conversations echoed around her, creating an atmosphere thick with tension. Today was her first follow-up appointment after her kidney cancer diagnosis, and she felt a whirlwind of emotions, nervousness, hope, and a hint of dread. It was a pivotal moment, one that would shape her understanding of her condition and the path ahead.

As she waited, Vanessa flipped through the pamphlets on the coffee table, each one highlighting different aspects of kidney cancer treatment and support. She tried to focus on the words, but her mind kept drifting. What would the doctor say? Would the news be good or bad? What if the treatment wasn't working? Each question was a reminder of the uncertainty that had become a constant companion since her diagnosis. She took a deep breath, reminding herself that she had come this far and that she was prepared to face whatever news awaited her.

When her name was finally called, Vanessa rose and followed the nurse down the hallway. The fluorescent lights above flickered slightly, and she felt a sense of surrealism wash over her. It was as if she were moving through a dream, one where the stakes were unfathomably high. As they entered the examination room, she noticed the clinical décor, white walls adorned with diagrams of the human body and a poster about healthy living. This was the place where decisions would be made, and she couldn't help but feel a sense of gravity settle around her.

Dr. Ramirez entered the room with a warm smile, his demeanor immediately putting her at ease. He greeted her with a firm handshake and motioned for her to take a seat. As he settled into his chair, Vanessa felt a surge of gratitude for his approachable nature. She had heard stories of doctors who were cold and clinical, but Dr. Ramirez had a way of making her feel like a partner in her care rather than just a patient. This was crucial, especially after the whirlwind of emotions she had experienced since her diagnosis.

"Vanessa, how have you been feeling since we last met?" he asked, his eyes attentive and sincere. She appreciated the way he genuinely wanted to know about her well-being, not just her physical symptoms. As she recounted her experiences over the past weeks,the fatigue, the weight fluctuations, the emotional roller coaster, she felt a weight lift off her shoulders. Speaking about her journey allowed her to process the tumult of her feelings, and she could see Dr. Ramirez nodding in understanding.

After listening carefully, Dr. Ramirez began to explain the results of her recent scans and blood work. The room felt charged with anticipation as he pulled up the images on his computer screen. He pointed out the areas of concern and explained what each scan revealed, using terms that were both technical and accessible. Vanessa focused intently on his words, trying to absorb the information while keeping her emotions in check. He emphasized that while there were challenges ahead, there was also room for optimism, noting that the early detection of her cancer had been crucial in determining a treatment plan.

As they discussed her treatment options, Vanessa felt a sense of empowerment wash over her. Dr. Ramirez laid out a comprehensive plan that included a combination of targeted therapy and immunotherapy, designed to combat the cancer while minimizing side effects. It was a relief to know that there were viable paths forward, and she felt a renewed sense of hope for her future. The idea of taking an active role in her treatment resonated with her, and she was eager to learn more about each approach.

Despite the encouraging news, Vanessa couldn't help but voice her concerns. "What about the side effects? How will this impact my daily life?" she asked, her voice trembling slightly. Dr. Ramirez acknowledged her fears, explaining that treatment could indeed be challenging but that they would work together to manage any side effects that arose. He reassured her that many patients found ways to cope and adapt, and that support networks would be available to help her through the toughest times. His compassion and understanding made her feel less isolated in her fears.

As the consultation continued, Vanessa realized how important it was to have open communication with her doctor. She asked about alternatives, lifestyle changes, and even complementary therapies that could support her treatment. Dr. Ramirez welcomed her questions, encouraging her to be proactive in her care. This collaborative approach brought Vanessa a sense of control amidst the chaos, reminding her that she was not just a passive recipient of treatment but an active participant in her healing journey.

Before the appointment concluded, Dr. Ramirez emphasized the importance of regular check-ins and monitoring her progress. He explained that her treatment would be tailored as they assessed how her body responded to the therapies. Vanessa felt a wave of relief at this personalized approach; it reassured her that she wouldn't be alone in this journey. As the doctor printed out a summary of their discussion, he encouraged her to take the time she needed to process the information and to reach out with any questions or concerns. Vanessa felt an overwhelming sense of gratitude wash over her. For the first time since her diagnosis, she felt equipped with a plan and a supportive ally in her corner.

Leaving the office, Vanessa found herself surrounded by the bustling energy of the hospital. The contrast between the vibrant, frenetic world outside and the heavy emotions she had been grappling with inside made her feel somewhat disoriented. She took a moment to breathe deeply, allowing the fresh air to invigorate her. As she walked to her car, she replayed the conversation with Dr. Ramirez in her mind, each detail bringing clarity to her earlier confusion. She was ready to take on the world, one step at a time.

Once in her car, Vanessa pulled out her phone and began drafting a message to her family and close friends. She wanted to share the news of her appointment and the treatment plan they had discussed. As she typed, her heart swelled with hope, and she realized how essential her support system had become. The love and encouragement she received from her loved ones were a crucial part of her healing process, and she felt an overwhelming desire to keep them informed and involved.

After sending the message, Vanessa decided to take a detour on her way home. She drove to a nearby park, a place that had always brought her peace. As she stepped out of her car and walked along the winding paths, she noticed the vibrant colors of the autumn leaves, the way the sunlight sparkled through the trees. It was a stark reminder that life continued to unfold, even in the face of challenges. She found solace in the beauty around her, allowing it to ground her amidst the uncertainty of her diagnosis.

Settling onto a bench, Vanessa closed her eyes and took a moment to reflect on her journey. It was so easy to get lost in the heaviness of her diagnosis, but today, she felt a glimmer of hope. She thought about the resilience she had witnessed in others who had faced cancer, the stories of triumph and courage that inspired her to fight. With each breath, she resolved to embrace her journey with the same determination, recognizing that she had the power to shape her experience.

As the sun began to set, casting a warm glow over the park, Vanessa pulled out her journal. Writing had become a therapeutic outlet for her, a way to process her thoughts and emotions. She began to jot down her feelings about the appointment, the mix of fear and hope that had accompanied her. She wrote about her commitment to self-care, the importance of surrounding herself with positivity, and her determination to fight this battle with every ounce of strength she possessed.

Returning home that evening, Vanessa felt lighter than she had in days. The weight of uncertainty still lingered, but it was no longer all-consuming. She had a plan, a supportive doctor, and a network of love and encouragement. As she prepared a simple dinner, she reflected on the importance of nourishing her body, both physically and emotionally. She decided to make a conscious effort to incorporate healthier meals into her routine, understanding that taking care of herself was paramount during this journey.

After dinner, she settled onto the couch with her laptop, eager to connect with others in the kidney cancer community. She discovered online forums and support groups where individuals shared their stories, tips, and encouragement. The sense of camaraderie was palpable, and Vanessa felt a deep connection to those who understood her struggles. She began to share her own journey, finding strength in vulnerability and the realization that she was not alone in this fight.

In the days that followed, Vanessa stuck to her new routine, balancing her treatment plan with self-care practices. She incorporated meditation and yoga into her mornings, finding solace in the quiet moments of reflection. Each day brought new challenges, but she approached them with a renewed sense of purpose. She began to record her thoughts in her journal more frequently, documenting the highs and lows of her experience, and celebrating small victories along the way.

As her treatment commenced, Vanessa embraced the journey with an open heart and a fierce determination. She found strength in her vulnerability, recognizing that it was okay to feel scared or uncertain. Each appointment with Dr. Ramirez became an opportunity for her to ask questions, seek guidance, and reaffirm her commitment to fighting this battle. She was learning to navigate the complexities of her diagnosis, and with every step, she felt herself growing stronger and more resilient.

Ultimately, Vanessa's journey was not just about battling kidney cancer; it was about rediscovering herself and the power of resilience. She learned that even in the face of adversity, there was beauty to be found in the connections she forged and the lessons she embraced. With each passing day, she became not just a survivor but a warrior, ready to face whatever challenges lay ahead with courage and strength.

Chapter Four

A Life-Altering Diagnosis

Vanessa's life was forever altered the moment she received the diagnosis of kidney cancer. The news felt like a punch to the gut, leaving her breathless and disoriented. Just weeks prior, she had been navigating the daily rhythms of her life, working at her job, spending time with friends and family, and enjoying her favorite hobbies. The sudden shift from ordinary to extraordinary was overwhelming. As she sat in the doctor's office, the weight of the words "kidney cancer" hung in the air, and she struggled to process the gravity of the situation. In that moment, her future felt uncertain, shrouded in fear and anxiety.

In the days that followed, Vanessa experienced a tumult of emotions, fear, anger, sadness, and confusion. The reality of her diagnosis seeped into every corner of her life, transforming her perspective. Simple moments, such as enjoying a cup of coffee in the morning or taking a walk in the park, were now tinged with the awareness of her mortality. Questions raced through her mind. How would this affect her relationships? Could she continue to pursue her passions? The once-familiar landscape of her life had shifted, and she felt like a stranger in her own skin.

However, amid the initial chaos, Vanessa began to find clarity. She realized that while cancer had changed her life, it did not have to define her. This diagnosis ignited a fierce determination within her to fight back and reclaim her narrative. She started researching her condition extensively, gathering information about treatment options and connecting with others who had faced similar battles. Each step she took toward understanding her illness empowered her, transforming her fear into a sense of agency. Vanessa began to see this as a journey, one that would challenge her but also reveal her strength and resilience.

As she navigated the complexities of her diagnosis, Vanessa discovered the importance of community and support. Friends and family rallied around her, offering encouragement and love, reminding her that she was not alone in this fight. She began to share her journey openly, using her story to inspire others while also seeking solace in shared experiences. This newfound sense of connection became a lifeline, reinforcing her belief that even in the face of adversity, there was hope, healing, and a profound sense of purpose waiting to be uncovered. In the throes of uncertainty, Vanessa was not just battling kidney cancer; she was rediscovering herself and the power of human connection in ways she had never imagined.

As the days turned into weeks, Vanessa immersed herself in a new routine that revolved around her health and well-being. She made a conscious effort to prioritize self-care, incorporating healthy eating, regular exercise, and mindfulness practices into her daily life. The act of preparing nutritious meals became a form of therapy for her, a way to nurture her body and reclaim a sense of control amidst the chaos. Each meal was not just sustenance, it was a symbol of her commitment to fight back against the cancer that threatened to derail her life.

In addition to her physical health, Vanessa began to explore emotional and spiritual healing. She enrolled in yoga that focused on restorative practices, which helped her find peace and tranquility in the midst of the storm. The gentle movements and guided meditations offered her a sanctuary where she could quiet her racing thoughts and connect with her inner self. With each session, she felt a little more grounded, a little more capable of facing the challenges ahead. The class became a safe space where she could release her fears and embrace the power of the present moment.

Vanessa also sought out support groups, both online and in-person, where she could share her experiences and learn from others who were on similar journeys. Hearing stories of survival and resilience from fellow cancer warriors inspired her beyond measure. She realized that everyone had their own unique battles, and yet, there was a shared bond that transcended their individual struggles. These connections fostered a sense of belonging, reminding her that she was part of a larger community of fighters. In this space, she felt understood and empowered, and she began to forge friendships that would last long after treatment.

As the months went by, Vanessa's perspective on life began to shift profoundly. The diagnosis that had once filled her with dread became a catalyst for transformation. She started to view each day as a gift, an opportunity to embrace life fully, regardless of the uncertainties that lay ahead. Simple joys,like a sunny afternoon spent with friends or a quiet evening reading a good book, now felt more significant and cherished. This newfound appreciation for the little things helped her cultivate gratitude, a powerful tool in her healing process.

Yet, not every day was easy. There were moments when fear would creep back in, threatening to overshadow her newfound optimism. During those times, Vanessa leaned on her support system, reaching out to friends and family who had become her anchors. She learned that it was okay to be vulnerable and to express her fears. Sharing her anxieties with those she trusted allowed her to release the weight of her worries and reminded her that she didn't have to face this journey alone. The strength she found in vulnerability became a source of resilience, helping her navigate the emotional roller coaster of her diagnosis.

Vanessa also began journaling regularly, using writing as a tool to process her thoughts and emotions. In her journal, she poured out her heart, documenting her fears, hopes, and dreams. Writing became a form of catharsis, allowing her to articulate feelings that were often difficult to express verbally. She found solace in the act of putting pen to paper, and as she reflected on her journey, she began to recognize the growth that had taken place within her. The pages were filled with both struggles and triumphs, a testament to her evolving relationship with her diagnosis.

As she continued her treatment, Vanessa became increasingly engaged in her health care decisions. She developed a strong partnership with her medical team, asking questions and seeking clarity on every aspect of her treatment plan. This proactive approach empowered her, providing a sense of agency in what could easily feel like a disempowering situation. Dr. Ramirez appreciated her involvement and encouraged her to voice any concerns or preferences regarding her care. With each conversation, Vanessa felt more equipped to navigate the complexities of her diagnosis, reinforcing her belief in her ability to overcome.

In the midst of her journey, Vanessa discovered a passion for advocacy. She began volunteering with local organizations that focused on cancer awareness and support. Sharing her story with others became a source of strength for her, and she felt compelled to help others who were facing similar challenges. Whether it was speaking at events or participating in fundraising efforts, she found immense fulfillment in being a voice for those who might feel unheard. This newfound purpose not only allowed her to give back but also helped her process her own experience in a meaningful way.

As she ventured further into her advocacy work, Vanessa connected with others who had turned their own battles into missions of hope. She was inspired by individuals who had created platforms to educate others about kidney cancer, and she began to dream of doing something similar. Vanessa envisioned creating a blog or a social media presence where she could share her journey, offer insights, and foster a sense of community among those affected by cancer. The idea excited her, and she felt a renewed sense of purpose taking shape as she considered how to leverage her experience to uplift others.

Months later, with a clear vision in mind, Vanessa launched her article. Each post became a canvas for her thoughts, emotions, and insights, capturing her journey through the highs and lows of living with kidney cancer. She shared her experiences candidly, from the challenges of treatment to the small victories that brought her joy. Her writing resonated with others who found themselves in similar situations, creating a vibrant community of support and understanding. As the article gained traction, Vanessa received messages from readers expressing gratitude for her openness and honesty, and she realized the profound impact her words were having on others. This realization fueled her passion even more; she understood that her story could inspire hope and resilience in those who felt isolated in their struggles. With every entry, she reaffirmed her belief that sharing one's journey could be a powerful catalyst for healing, both for herself and for those who followed along.

Chapter Five

Understanding Kidney Cancer

Vanessa's journey of understanding kidney cancer began with a personal connection. When her uncle was diagnosed with renal cell carcinoma, she found herself thrust into a world filled with medical jargon, treatment options, and emotional turmoil. Initially, she felt overwhelmed by the sheer volume of information available. The term 'kidney cancer' alone encompassed various types and subtypes, including clear cell carcinoma, papillary carcinoma, and chromophobe carcinoma. Each type differed in behavior, treatment, and prognosis, making it crucial for Vanessa to grasp the nuances of the disease.

As Vanessa delved deeper into her research, she discovered the risk factors associated with kidney cancer. It became evident that certain lifestyle choices could increase one's risk, such as smoking, obesity, and high blood pressure. Genetic predispositions also played a significant role, as she learned about syndromes like von Hippel-Lindau disease that could elevate the likelihood of developing kidney tumors. This knowledge made her acutely aware of the importance of prevention and early detection, as she began to reflect on her own lifestyle choices and family history.

The symptoms of kidney cancer were another area where Vanessa sought clarity. She was surprised to learn that the disease could often be asymptomatic in its early stages. However, when symptoms did manifest, they could include blood in the urine, persistent back pain, and unexplained weight loss. This realization was sobering; many people might ignore these signs, attributing them to less serious conditions. It highlighted the importance of regular check-ups and being vigilant about one's health, especially for individuals with risk factors.

Understanding the staging of kidney cancer was a pivotal moment for Vanessa. She learned that the disease is classified into stages based on tumor size and whether it has spread to nearby lymph nodes or distant organs. This staging system directly influenced treatment options and prognosis. For instance, stage I kidney cancer, where the tumor is small and localized, often has a much better prognosis than stage IV, where the cancer has metastasized. Vanessa recognized that early diagnosis could significantly impact survival rates, emphasizing the need for awareness and education.

As she continued her research, Vanessa explored the various treatment options available for kidney cancer. She learned about surgical interventions, such as nephrectomy, where the affected kidney is removed. Additionally, she discovered that for some patients, targeted therapies and immunotherapies could be effective, particularly for advanced stages of the disease. This information brought a sense of hope, as she realized that advancements in medical science were providing patients with more options than ever before.

Vanessa also became attuned to the emotional and psychological aspects of dealing with kidney cancer. She understood that a cancer diagnosis not only affected the physical health of the patient but also had profound implications for their mental well-being. Support systems, whether through family, friends, or support groups, became critical components of coping with the disease. Vanessa appreciated the importance of mental health resources, realizing that patients should not only focus on physical treatment but also nurture their emotional resilience.

During her research, Vanessa stumbled upon the significance of clinical trials in the fight against kidney cancer. She learned that these trials often provide patients with access to cutting-edge treatments that are not yet widely available. Participating in a clinical trial could be a viable option for those with advanced stages of the disease or for those who had exhausted other treatment avenues. This information empowered Vanessa, as she recognized the role of research in improving outcomes for future patients.

In her quest for understanding, Vanessa also found numerous organizations dedicated to kidney cancer awareness and research. These organizations played a vital role in funding research, providing resources for patients and families, and advocating for better treatment options. Vanessa felt inspired by the stories of survivors and resilience shared by these organizations. She realized that awareness and education were crucial in changing the narrative around kidney cancer, fostering a community of support and hope.

Through her exploration, Vanessa became aware of the disparities in kidney cancer treatment and outcomes among different populations. Factors such as socioeconomic status, access to healthcare, and cultural attitudes towards cancer could significantly influence diagnosis and treatment. This realization opened her eyes to the importance of addressing these disparities to ensure that all patients received the care they deserved, regardless of their background.

As Vanessa reflected on her newfound understanding of kidney cancer, she felt a sense of responsibility to share this knowledge with others. She began organizing informational sessions at her local community center, aiming to educate others about the disease, its risk factors, and the importance of early detection. By empowering her community with information, Vanessa hoped to promote a proactive approach to health and wellness, ensuring that others could benefit from the lessons she had learned.

Ultimately, Vanessa's understanding of kidney cancer transcended mere facts and figures; it became a narrative of hope, resilience, and community. Her experience taught her the value of education in combating fear and misinformation surrounding cancer. By fostering awareness and encouraging open discussions about kidney cancer, Vanessa aimed to break the stigma associated with the disease and inspire others to take charge of their health. Through her efforts, Vanessa envisioned a future where knowledge about kidney cancer could lead to early detection and improved outcomes for all affected individuals. She recognized that, while medical advancements were critical, the human element—support, understanding, and education—was equally vital in the fight against cancer. This realization motivated her to collaborate with local healthcare providers to create resources tailored to her community's needs, ensuring that information was accessible and relatable.

During her outreach initiatives, Vanessa learned to appreciate the diverse experiences of those living with kidney cancer. Each story she encountered was unique, shaped by individual circumstances, backgrounds, and coping mechanisms. By listening to these narratives, she began to understand the complex emotional landscape that accompanies a cancer diagnosis. This empathy allowed her to connect more deeply with the individuals and families she aimed to support, fostering a sense of community and solidarity among those impacted.

As Vanessa expanded her knowledge, she also began to explore the role of nutrition and lifestyle changes in managing kidney cancer. Research suggested that a balanced diet rich in fruits, vegetables, and whole grains could potentially improve overall health and well-being, offering patients a sense of control over their circumstances. She began to incorporate this information into her sessions, emphasizing the importance of holistic care that addressed not only the physical aspects of the disease but also the emotional and nutritional needs of patients.

One of Vanessa's most rewarding experiences was organizing a community health fair focused on kidney cancer awareness. The event brought together healthcare professionals, survivors, and advocates to share information and resources. Attendees had the opportunity to participate in workshops, ask questions, and receive free screenings. The positive feedback from participants reinforced Vanessa's belief in the power of community engagement and education in tackling health issues. It was a testament to the idea that knowledge is not just power; it is a path to healing and hope.

In her journey, Vanessa also encountered the importance of advocacy. She began to understand the role that policy and funding play in kidney cancer research and treatment. By engaging with local lawmakers and health organizations, she advocated for increased research funding and better access to care for affected individuals. This newfound sense of purpose galvanized her commitment to making a difference, as she realized that advocacy could lead to tangible changes in the healthcare landscape.

As Vanessa continued her work, she felt a personal transformation. The fear and uncertainty that initially accompanied her uncle's diagnosis had evolved into a sense of empowerment and purpose. She recognized that while kidney cancer could be a devastating diagnosis, it also provided an opportunity for communities to come together, share experiences, and support one another. This perspective shift helped her cultivate a more hopeful outlook, both for herself and for those she sought to help.

The relationships she built through her outreach work became a cornerstone of her understanding of kidney cancer. Vanessa found that connecting with survivors and their families enriched her knowledge and fueled her passion. These personal connections not only informed her advocacy efforts but also deepened her appreciation for the resilience of those facing the challenges of cancer. Each shared story added a layer of understanding to her awareness of the emotional and psychological toll of the disease.

As Vanessa's advocacy gained momentum, she began leveraging social media platforms to reach a broader audience. She created an online community dedicated to sharing information about kidney cancer, where individuals could find resources, ask questions, and share their experiences. This digital space became a sanctuary for many, allowing them to connect with others who understood their struggles and triumphs. Vanessa recognized the power of social media in amplifying voices and fostering a sense of belonging among those touched by kidney cancer.

Through these efforts, Vanessa became a local advocate for kidney cancer awareness, earning recognition for her commitment to education and support. She was invited to speak at conferences and events, where she shared her journey and the importance of community in combating cancer. With each speaking engagement, she felt a renewed sense of purpose, knowing that her story could inspire others to take action and be proactive about their health.

Ultimately, Vanessa's understanding of kidney cancer transformed her life in profound ways. What began as a personal struggle evolved into a mission to empower others, fostering a culture of awareness, support, and resilience. She realized that knowledge could be a powerful tool in the fight against cancer, equipping individuals with the information they needed to navigate their health journeys. As she looked to the future, Vanessa remained committed to her advocacy efforts, hopeful that her work would contribute to a world where kidney cancer could be detected early, treated effectively, and ultimately, overcome.

In the end, Vanessa understood that while kidney cancer was a formidable opponent, the strength of community, education, and support could make all the difference. Through her journey, she not only transformed her own understanding but also inspired others to join the fight against kidney cancer. Together, they could create a legacy of hope, resilience, and empowerment, ensuring that no one had to face the challenges of kidney cancer alone.

Chapter Six

Facing the Unknown

When Vanessa first learned that she had kidney cancer, she was enveloped by a wave of fear and uncertainty. It was a typical day when she noticed persistent back pain and a sense of fatigue that wouldn't go away. Initially, she brushed it off, attributing it to stress from work and personal life responsibilities. However, as the weeks progressed, her symptoms did not improve. After a series of tests and imaging, the news came like a thunderclap: she had a kidney tumor. The doctor's voice was calm, but the words felt heavy, leaving Vanessa grappling with the reality of her diagnosis.

The subsequent appointment revealed that the tumor's size was astonishing, eight pounds. Hearing this, Vanessa felt a mix of disbelief and dread. She had read about kidney tumors but never imagined she would be facing one of the largest the doctor had ever encountered. It put everything into perspective; how could something so massive exist within her without her awareness? The thought was both terrifying and surreal. This was not just a medical condition to her; it was an invasion of her body, and the unknowns surrounding it felt insurmountable.

As Vanessa sat in the sterile examination room, staring at the medical diagrams and images of her tumor, she felt a surge of emotions. Questions flooded her mind: How did this happen? What would the treatment entail? Would she be able to recover? The doctor provided information on the next steps, including potential surgery to remove the tumor, but the details felt overwhelming. Vanessa realized she was not just facing a physical battle; she was also wrestling with the emotional turmoil of facing an uncertain future.

In the days that followed, Vanessa found herself oscillating between hope and despair. Researching kidney cancer and learning about her specific type of tumor became a coping mechanism. She discovered that while her tumor was large, many patients had successfully undergone treatment and emerged stronger. However, the sheer size of her tumor still loomed over her thoughts, creating a constant reminder of the battle she was about to face. It was a daunting task to balance the information she found online with the realities of her situation.

As she navigated this tumultuous period, Vanessa leaned heavily on her support system. Family and friends rallied around her, providing emotional support and practical assistance. She found comfort in their presence, as they listened to her fears and offered encouragement. Yet, she also realized that they could not fully understand the weight of her experience. The journey of facing a kidney cancer diagnosis, especially one involving such a large tumor, was profoundly personal, and at times she felt isolated in her struggle.

Determined not to succumb to fear, Vanessa began to take control of her situation. She sought out multiple opinions from specialists and engaged in discussions about her treatment options. The idea of surgery was both terrifying and liberating; it represented a potential path to reclaiming her health. In her research, she learned about the advances in surgical techniques, including minimally invasive procedures, which provided a glimmer of hope. The more informed she became, the more empowered she felt to make decisions about her care.

Vanessa also found solace in journaling her thoughts and feelings throughout this journey. Writing became a therapeutic outlet, allowing her to articulate her fears, hopes, and frustrations. She documented her experiences, from the initial diagnosis to the various appointments and consultations. This process helped her process the overwhelming emotions and provided a sense of clarity amidst the chaos. It was a reminder that she was not just a patient; she was a fighter, and she had the agency to navigate this journey on her terms.

As her surgery date approached, Vanessa began to confront the reality of her situation with a mixture of anxiety and resolve. The idea of undergoing such a significant procedure to remove the eight-pound tumor was daunting, but she also felt a sense of urgency. The larger the tumor, the more pressing the need for intervention. With each passing day, she focused on cultivating a positive mindset, visualizing herself as a survivor who would emerge from this experience stronger and more resilient.

On the day of the surgery, Vanessa was filled with a sense of calm determination. She had surrounded herself with positivity in the days leading up to the procedure, and it had helped quell her fears. As she was wheeled into the operating room, she took a deep breath and reminded herself of the support she had and the journey she was embarking on. The surgical team was reassuring, and their expertise gave her confidence that she was in capable hands.

Post-surgery, Vanessa awoke to the reality of her new life. The eight-pound tumor had been successfully removed, and while she faced a long road of recovery ahead, she felt an immense sense of relief. The burden of the unknown had shifted; she was no longer living with the weight of the tumor, both physically and emotionally. Instead, she was now focused on healing and rebuilding her strength. The support from her loved ones continued to uplift her, and she felt an overwhelming sense of gratitude for their unwavering presence throughout her journey. Each visit from family and friends provided a reminder that she was not alone in this fight. Their encouragement fueled her determination to embrace the recovery process, and Vanessa began to see each small milestone as a victory. Whether it was taking her first steps post-surgery or managing to eat a full meal, each achievement reminded her of the strength she possessed.

As the days turned into weeks, Vanessa found herself slowly regaining her strength. Physical therapy sessions became a routine, and though they were often challenging, she approached them with the same resolve that had guided her through the diagnosis and surgery. The therapists were encouraging, helping her to set realistic goals and celebrating every inch of progress. With each session, she became more aware of her body's capabilities and the resilience it held within. She realized that while the journey was arduous, it was also an opportunity for growth and self-discovery.

During this recovery period, Vanessa also took time to reflect on her experience and the lessons it had taught her. She began to understand that facing the unknown was not just about grappling with fear; it was also about embracing vulnerability. The journey had stripped away some of her previous certainties and forced her to reevaluate what truly mattered. Family, health, and connection took precedence over the mundane worries that once consumed her. This shift in perspective was perhaps one of the most valuable outcomes of her ordeal.

With her physical health gradually improving, Vanessa felt compelled to share her story with others. She wanted to raise awareness about kidney cancer, particularly the importance of early detection and treatment. She began to participate in local support groups, both as a survivor and as an advocate. Speaking openly about her experience, including the shock of discovering her tumor's size, resonated with many who attended. Vanessa's story became a beacon of hope for those facing similar battles, proving that strength can emerge from even the darkest of times.

In sharing her journey, Vanessa also discovered the power of community. The connections she formed with fellow survivors and their families enriched her understanding of kidney cancer's broader impact. Each shared experience added depth to her advocacy, reminding her that everyone's journey was unique yet interconnected. Through group discussions, she learned about the various challenges others faced, from navigating treatment options to dealing with the emotional toll of a cancer diagnosis. This sense of solidarity fueled her passion for spreading awareness.

As the months passed, Vanessa became increasingly involved in kidney cancer research initiatives. She collaborated with local organizations to help fundraise for research and support programs. Her passion was infectious, inspiring others in her community to become involved. Whether it was organizing charity runs or educational workshops, Vanessa dedicated herself to creating an impact that extended beyond her personal journey. She understood that raising awareness could lead to earlier diagnoses and better outcomes for others, and that became her mission.

Through her advocacy work, Vanessa also cultivated a sense of empowerment that had previously eluded her. The experience of facing a daunting challenge, overcoming it, and then helping others navigate similar paths instilled a newfound confidence. She realized that her voice mattered and that sharing her story could influence change. This realization spurred her to write articles and contribute to online platforms dedicated to cancer awareness, ensuring that her message reached a wider audience.

In her personal life, the aftermath of her kidney cancer battle brought her closer to her loved ones. The shared experience of supporting her through her diagnosis and recovery had strengthened their bonds. Vanessa cherished the moments spent with family and friends, recognizing that life's unpredictability made each moment precious. She also took the time to reconnect with herself, exploring new hobbies and interests that she had previously set aside. The freedom to enjoy life beyond cancer was liberating, and she embraced it wholeheartedly.

As she continued her journey, Vanessa also became an advocate for mental health awareness. She recognized that navigating a cancer diagnosis was not just a physical battle; it was also a profound emotional journey. She began to speak about the importance of seeking support for mental health, encouraging others to address their feelings and fears openly. Whether through therapy, support groups, or creative outlets, Vanessa highlighted that taking care of one's mental well-being was just as crucial as managing physical health.

Through her advocacy and personal growth, Vanessa found a renewed sense of purpose. The experience of facing an eight-pound tumor and emerging on the other side had transformed her in ways she could not have anticipated. She had discovered her strength, resilience, and the power of community. As she looked toward the future, Vanessa felt a profound sense of hope. She knew that while uncertainties would always exist, she had the tools and support to navigate whatever challenges lay ahead.

Ultimately, Vanessa's journey became a testament to the human spirit's capacity to rise above adversity. She had faced the unknown, confronted her fears, and emerged not just as a survivor but as an advocate and a source of inspiration for others. The experience of battling kidney cancer had redefined her understanding of life, love, and connection.

Chapter Seven

The Research Begins

Vanessa's journey with kidney cancer began with an unexpected diagnosis that turned her world upside down. For months, she had been experiencing vague symptoms such as fatigue and occasional pain in her lower back. After a series of doctor visits and tests, she received the shocking news: an eight-pound tumor was residing in her kidney. The size and aggression of the tumor left her in disbelief, but she was determined to fight back. With the support of her family and friends, Vanessa underwent surgery to remove the tumor, marking what she hoped would be the end of her cancer journey.

However, the relief of having the tumor removed was short-lived. Shortly after her surgery, Vanessa began to experience new symptoms that were increasingly alarming. A series of scans revealed that the cancer had metastasized, spreading to her lymph nodes and even her brain. This news felt like a crushing blow; the very thought of her body being invaded by cancer cells again was almost too much to bear. Vanessa found herself grappling with a new reality, one that was filled with uncertainty and fear. The vigor of her fight against cancer had intensified, and she knew she had to muster every ounce of courage to face this new challenge.

As she began her journey into treatment for metastatic kidney cancer, Vanessa immersed herself in research. She became a student of her own illness, combing through medical journals, clinical trials, and survivor stories. She learned that understanding her cancer was essential to navigating her treatment options. Vanessa discovered that targeted therapies and immunotherapies were emerging as promising treatments for metastatic kidney cancer, offering her a glimmer of hope. The more she educated herself, the more empowered she felt to engage with her medical team in discussions about her care.

Despite the emotional toll of her diagnosis, Vanessa found solace in connecting with others who were facing similar battles. She joined support groups where individuals shared their experiences, fears, and triumphs. These connections provided her with a sense of community and understanding that she desperately needed. Hearing stories of resilience and hope from other cancer warriors inspired her to remain optimistic. Vanessa understood that she was not alone in this fight; there were many others who had walked similar paths and emerged stronger.

Throughout her treatment, Vanessa faced a myriad of physical and emotional challenges. The side effects of chemotherapy and radiation were daunting, often leaving her exhausted and disheartened. Yet, she was resolute in her commitment to push through. Her daily routine transformed into a regimen of medications, appointments, and self-care practices. She prioritized her mental health, incorporating meditation and mindfulness into her life, which helped her cope with the anxiety that often accompanied her diagnosis. Vanessa learned the importance of nurturing her spirit, recognizing that mental fortitude was as crucial as physical strength in her battle.

As the months progressed, Vanessa faced additional hurdles. The cancer treatments took a toll on her body, leading to significant weight loss and the loss of her hair. She grappled with feelings of inadequacy and despair, questioning her identity beyond being a cancer patient. However, she also discovered a newfound appreciation for her body and its ability to endure. Vanessa began documenting her journey through a blog, sharing her experiences with others and providing insights into the emotional and physical complexities of living with cancer. Her vulnerability resonated with many, and she found comfort in the stories of those who followed her journey.

In her quest for healing, Vanessa also sought alternative therapies. She explored nutritional changes, incorporating a plant-based diet rich in antioxidants and anti-inflammatory foods. She participated in yoga classes designed for cancer patients, finding peace and strength in movement. These holistic approaches complemented her medical treatments, allowing her to feel more in control of her health. By embracing a comprehensive approach to her well-being, Vanessa discovered that healing could encompass more than just traditional medicine; it could also involve nurturing her mind, body, and spirit.

As the treatment continued, Vanessa encountered moments of progress and setbacks. Scans would sometimes show promising results, only for new complications to arise. The emotional rollercoaster was exhausting, yet she leaned on her support network for encouragement. Family and friends rallied around her, organizing fundraisers to help cover medical expenses and providing practical assistance during her toughest days. Vanessa realized that allowing others to support her was not a sign of weakness; rather, it was an expression of love and community that fortified her resolve.

Amidst the chaos, Vanessa also found herself reflecting on her life and priorities. The cancer diagnosis prompted her to reevaluate what truly mattered to her. She cultivated deeper relationships, engaged in meaningful conversations, and sought to experience life to its fullest. Each day became an opportunity for gratitude, and she learned to savor the small moments. Whether it was enjoying a cup of tea while watching the sunrise or spending quality time with loved ones, Vanessa embraced the beauty of the present.

In her ongoing fight against cancer, Vanessa became an advocate for awareness and research funding. She participated in local cancer walks and events, sharing her story to inspire others to take action and contribute to the cause. Vanessa understood that raising awareness about kidney cancer was crucial in promoting early detection and better treatment options for future patients. She collaborated with cancer organizations, sharing her insights and experiences at community events to educate others on the importance of recognizing symptoms and seeking timely medical advice. The more she spoke out, the more she felt a sense of purpose, transforming her personal struggle into a collective call to action.

Through her advocacy work, Vanessa also connected with researchers and healthcare professionals dedicated to advancing treatment options for metastatic kidney cancer. She participated in focus groups and provided patient input on clinical trials, believing that her experiences could help shape future research initiatives. Vanessa was determined to contribute to the scientific community's understanding of the disease, hoping that one day her efforts would lead to breakthroughs that could save lives. Every conversation and every piece of feedback was a step toward improving the landscape for those who would follow in her footsteps.

As the months turned into years, Vanessa's health fluctuated, yet she remained steadfast in her resolve. There were moments of stability where her scans showed no new growth, providing her with a temporary reprieve from the looming shadow of her illness. These moments were precious, and she celebrated them with gratitude and joy. Yet, there were also instances when the cancer would rear its head again, bringing with it fear and uncertainty. Each time, Vanessa leaned into her coping strategies, reminding herself of the strength she had cultivated over her journey.

During this time, Vanessa also focused on her relationships. She made a concerted effort to connect with friends and family, often organizing gatherings that celebrated life, despite the darkness of her illness. These gatherings were filled with laughter, storytelling, and shared meals, creating an atmosphere of love and support. Vanessa recognized that being present with her loved ones was a gift, and she cherished every moment spent in their company. In doing so, she fostered connections that not only bolstered her spirits but also provided a network of support during her toughest days.

In her personal life, Vanessa found a new passion for writing. Inspired by her blog and the stories of others, she began drafting a memoir that chronicled her experiences with cancer. This endeavor became a therapeutic outlet, allowing her to process her emotions and reflect on the profound lessons she had learned. Writing provided a sense of clarity and purpose, and she hoped that her story could inspire others facing similar battles. Vanessa envisioned a future where her words could offer comfort and encouragement, reminding others that they were not alone in their struggles.

As time passed, Vanessa also saw advancements in the medical field that ignited her hope. New treatments and clinical trials emerged, offering innovative options for patients like her. She eagerly followed developments in kidney cancer research, often sharing updates with her support community. Vanessa felt a sense of pride in being part of a movement that was actively seeking to improve outcomes for cancer patients. The progress reassured her that the fight against cancer was ongoing and that every voice, including hers, contributed to the larger narrative of hope and resilience.

With a renewed sense of purpose, Vanessa decided to take her advocacy to a national level. She joined a coalition of cancer survivors and advocates, participating in lobbying efforts to increase funding for cancer research and support services. Her voice became a powerful tool in advocating for policy changes that would benefit patients across the country. Vanessa understood the importance of systemic change in the fight against cancer, and she was determined to be a part of that change. Each meeting and rally fueled her passion, reminding her that her experiences could influence the lives of many.

In the face of ongoing challenges, Vanessa prioritized self-care and mental well-being. She continued to practice mindfulness and meditation, finding solace in moments of stillness. She also explored creative outlets, such as painting and gardening, which provided her with joy and a sense of accomplishment. Vanessa learned that nurturing her interests beyond cancer allowed her to reclaim parts of her identity that she feared had been overshadowed by her illness. Each brushstroke and blooming flower symbolized her resilience and ability to find beauty amidst adversity.

As Vanessa looked to the future, she embraced a mindset of hope and determination. She understood that her journey with kidney cancer was not defined solely by her diagnosis but by her ability to rise above it. She cherished the relationships she had built, the lessons she had learned, and the advocacy work she had undertaken. Vanessa was committed to living life fully, savoring every moment, and continuing to share her story with the world. Her cancer journey was ongoing, but she was ready to face whatever lay ahead with courage and grace.

Ultimately, Vanessa's story became one of transformation. What began as a devastating diagnosis evolved into a powerful narrative of strength, hope, and advocacy. She emerged as a beacon of light for others, encouraging them to find their voices and fight for their health. In every challenge she faced, Vanessa discovered opportunities for growth and connection, proving that even in the darkest of times, one can find a path toward healing.

Chapter Eight

Building a Support Network

Despite the overwhelming fatigue that often accompanied her cancer treatments, Vanessa remained steadfast in her commitment to building a support network. She understood the importance of having a strong foundation of friends and family to lean on during her darkest moments. Even on days when she felt too exhausted to engage fully, she made an effort to reach out to her loved ones, organizing virtual meetups or small gatherings whenever her energy allowed. Vanessa learned that social connections were vital to her mental well-being, and they provided her with a sense of normalcy amidst the chaos of her diagnosis.

As she navigated this difficult period, Vanessa also found herself connecting with fellow cancer patients. She sought out online support groups and local meetups, where she met individuals who shared similar experiences. These connections helped her feel less isolated; they understood the unique challenges she faced and provided a space for her to express her fears and hopes. Vanessa was struck by the resilience of her new friends, many of whom were fighting their own battles with various forms of cancer. Their shared stories became a source of inspiration for her, reinforcing her belief that support was a two-way street.

Amidst the emotional turmoil of her journey, Vanessa received devastating news that would irrevocably change the course of her fight against cancer. After a routine scan, her oncologist delivered the news: the cancer had progressed significantly, and she was given only one month to live. The words hung heavily in the air, and Vanessa felt as if the ground had been pulled from beneath her. She was filled with disbelief, fear, and an overwhelming sense of urgency. The thought of leaving her loved ones behind was unbearable, yet she knew she had to harness every ounce of strength within her to face this challenge head-on.

In the midst of this crushing reality, Vanessa's medical team presented her with an opportunity that sparked a flicker of hope. They had recently begun using a new therapy called Radvax, which was still in experimental stages. The treatment aimed to enhance the body's immune response to cancer cells, and although it was not a guaranteed solution, it offered her a chance to prolong her life and fight back against the disease. Vanessa grappled with the decision, weighing the risks and potential benefits, but ultimately, she felt compelled to try anything that could give her more time with her family and friends.

With her decision made, Vanessa's support network rallied around her, providing both emotional and logistical assistance as she embarked on this new treatment. Friends organized meal trains, ensuring that she had nourishing food during her treatment days. Family members visited regularly, filling her home with love and laughter, reminding her of the life she was fighting to preserve. Vanessa felt an overwhelming sense of gratitude for the people in her life who stepped up during this critical time, and their unwavering support became a lifeline as she prepared for her upcoming treatments.

As Vanessa began her Radvax therapy, she experienced a mix of hope and anxiety. The treatment sessions were grueling, and she often felt fatigued and nauseous. Yet, she remained determined to focus on the positives. Each treatment brought with it the possibility of a new beginning, and Vanessa clung to that hope like a beacon of light in her darkest days. She documented her experiences, sharing updates with her support network through social media, which allowed her to feel connected and engaged even when she was physically drained.

During this tumultuous time, Vanessa also prioritized her mental health. She sought out counseling services tailored for cancer patients, where she could openly discuss her fears, dreams, and everything in between. These sessions provided a safe haven for her to express emotions that often felt too heavy to carry alone. Vanessa learned that addressing her mental health was just as crucial as her physical treatment, and she embraced the opportunity to work through her feelings with a professional who understood the complexities of her situation.

As the weeks went by, Vanessa began to notice subtle changes in her body. While she still battled significant fatigue, there were moments of clarity and strength that she hadn't felt in a long time. Encouraged by these small victories, she continued to participate in her support groups, sharing her journey and uplifting others in similar situations. Vanessa found purpose in her advocacy, reminding herself and her peers that every day was a gift, no matter the challenges they faced. Her story resonated with many, and she felt a renewed sense of purpose as she inspired others to find their own strength.

In the midst of her treatment, Vanessa also took the time to reflect on her life. She began to write letters to her loved ones, expressing her feelings, sharing memories, and imparting wisdom she hoped they would carry with them. This act of vulnerability allowed her to articulate her love and gratitude, creating lasting keepsakes for those she cherished. Writing became both a therapeutic outlet and a means of connecting with her family on a deeper level, ensuring that her voice would continue to resonate even after she was gone.

As Vanessa approached the end of her one-month prognosis, hope began to flourish within her. The Radvax therapy had thus far shown promising signs, and her doctors noted that her tumor markers were stabilizing. Although she still faced days filled with exhaustion, she was increasingly aware of her resilience. Each treatment brought with it a renewed sense of possibility; she was determined to make the most of the time she had left, refusing to let fear dictate her actions. With her support network firmly by her side, Vanessa was ready to embrace whatever came next.

Her friends organized a celebration of life gathering, a way to honor her journey and all the love she had shared with those around her. They decorated her home with bright flowers and photographs that represented milestones in her life, from childhood moments to recent adventures. The atmosphere was filled with warmth, laughter, and tears, blending joy and sorrow in a beautiful tapestry of human connection. Vanessa felt enveloped by the love of those who had walked alongside her, and in that moment, she realized that her life had been rich and full, no matter the challenges she faced.

The gathering allowed Vanessa to share her reflections and express her gratitude. She spoke about the lessons she had learned throughout her cancer journey—the importance of cherishing each day, finding joy in small moments, and nurturing relationships. As she looked around the room, she saw the faces of those who had supported her, and her heart swelled with appreciation. She encouraged everyone to embrace life fully, to laugh often and love deeply, and to carry her spirit with them as they navigated their own journeys.

In the days following the celebration, Vanessa focused on creating lasting memories. She organized small outings with her loved ones, whether it was a picnic at the park or a movie night at home. She relished these moments, capturing them with photographs and journal entries, knowing that each memory would serve as a treasure for her family and friends. Vanessa understood that while her time might be limited, the love and joy they shared would resonate long after her departure. These experiences became a source of strength and comfort for her.

As her treatment continued, Vanessa also spoke openly about her fears and uncertainties. She found solace in candid conversations with her support network, where vulnerability became a powerful tool for connection. By sharing her innermost thoughts, she created a safe space for others to voice their feelings as well. They discussed everything from their emotions about loss to their hopes for the future, fostering a collective understanding of the human experience. This openness deepened their bonds and made the journey feel less isolating.

Meanwhile, Vanessa's medical team continued to monitor her progress closely. The Radvax therapy was showing promising results, and there were discussions about extending her treatment plan. With each scan, Vanessa felt a mix of hope and anxiety. The prospect of more time was exhilarating, yet it also came with the burden of uncertainty. She grappled with the reality of her situation but chose to focus on the positives, reminding herself that every day granted her another opportunity to create memories and advocate for others facing similar battles.

In her advocacy efforts, Vanessa connected with local cancer organizations, sharing her story and pushing for greater awareness of kidney cancer. She participated in community events, raising funds for research and support services. Each time she spoke, she felt a surge of purpose, as if she were transforming her pain into something meaningful. Vanessa knew that her voice could help others navigate their own journeys, and she was determined to be a source of hope and inspiration for those who felt lost in their battles.

Simultaneously, Vanessa utilized her writing as a platform to reach a broader audience. She began to draft articles that highlighted the importance of early detection and support networks in battling cancer. Her words resonated with many, and she received messages from people around the country who had been touched by her story. Vanessa realized that her experiences could connect her with others, fostering a sense of community that transcended her immediate circle. This realization empowered her further, igniting a passion for advocacy that she had never fully explored before.

As the month progressed, Vanessa became increasingly attuned to her body and its needs. She adapted her self-care routine, incorporating practices such as gentle yoga and guided meditation. These activities helped her to manage stress and cultivate a sense of calm amidst the uncertainty. Vanessa found solace in her daily rituals, which became a grounding force in her life. She understood that taking care of her mental and physical well-being was crucial, especially as she navigated the complexities of her treatment and prognosis.

With the support of her family, friends, and healthcare team, Vanessa continued to approach each day with a spirit of gratitude and resilience. The love that surrounded her became a source of strength, empowering her to face whatever challenges lay ahead. She cherished the moments of connection—whether it was a heartfelt conversation, a shared meal, or a simple hug. In the face of uncertainty, Vanessa discovered that the human spirit is remarkably resilient, and she vowed to embrace the beauty of life.

Chapter Nine

The First Treatment Plan

Vanessa, had always been a fighter, but when she embarked on her first treatment plan involving Radvax therapy, she felt as if she were facing a foe unlike any other. Initially, she was filled with hope as she began the treatment, believing it would be her pathway to recovery. However, what followed was a grueling journey marked by an intense wave of sickness that left her feeling more vulnerable than ever. The side effects were relentless, and as each day passed, she found herself grappling with a profound sense of despair.

The Radvax therapy, designed to target the disease that had invaded her body, quickly revealed its darker side. Instead of healing, it seemed to launch an assault on her own physical structure, ravaging her cartilage and leaving her joints aching with an intensity that was hard to describe. As the pain grew, so did her frustration. Vanessa had always prided herself on her resilience, but the toll of the treatment began to chip away at her spirit, leading her to question her choices and wonder if the path she had chosen was truly the right one.

Amidst the physical turmoil, Vanessa was also battling an emotional storm. She found herself in a cycle of hope and despair-moments of optimism dashed by waves of nausea and pain. Each day felt like a new battle, one in which she had to muster every ounce of determination just to get out of bed. The reflection in the mirror showed a woman who was slowly being worn down, both physically and mentally, yet deep within her, a flicker of resilience remained. She knew she had to fight, not just for herself but for her loved ones who were rooting for her recovery.

As her body struggled under the weight of the therapy, Vanessa faced the prospect of further surgeries with a mixture of fear and resolve. The recommendation to have her thyroid removed loomed over her like a dark cloud. She understood that this procedure was necessary to combat the disease, but the thought of enduring more invasive treatment was daunting. The idea of being cut open again, of recovery periods and the accompanying pain, filled her with anxiety. Yet, as she weighed her options, she realized that her desire to live was stronger than her fear.

Despite the setbacks, Vanessa sought to find strength in her struggle. She began to document her journey, pouring her thoughts and emotions onto the pages of a journal. Writing became a therapeutic outlet, allowing her to process the chaos that surrounded her. Through her words, she captured the essence of her fight-the moments of vulnerability interspersed with bursts of hope. This practice not only provided her with clarity but also helped her connect with others who were facing similar battles, reminding her that she was not alone.

During this tumultuous time, the support of her family and friends proved to be invaluable. They rallied around her, providing a network of love and encouragement that served as a lifeline. Each visit, phone call, and message became a source of comfort, reminding Vanessa of the life she was fighting for. Their unwavering belief in her strength bolstered her resolve, and she found herself drawing energy from their faith in her ability to overcome. She realized that this journey was not just hers; it was a collective struggle, and their support made it a little bit easier to bear.

As Vanessa prepared for her upcoming surgery, she focused on cultivating a mindset of positivity. She surrounded herself with uplifting books, inspirational quotes, and stories of survival. Each piece of encouragement became a stepping stone on her path to healing. She visualized the surgery as a necessary step toward reclaiming her health and envisioned a future where she could once again embrace life fully. By mentally preparing herself for the challenges ahead, she aimed to build a fortress of strength around her fragile spirit.

The day of the surgery arrived, and Vanessa felt a swirl of emotions-fear, hope, and determination coalescing into a singular purpose. As she lay on the operating table, she closed her eyes and envisioned herself emerging victorious from this experience. In that moment, she surrendered to the process, trusting in the skills of the medical team and the resilience of her own body. The surgery was both a physical and emotional turning point, a chapter that she hoped would lead her closer to a life unburdened by the weight of illness.

Post-surgery, the recovery process was fraught with its own challenges. The pain was intense, and there were days when Vanessa questioned her decision to undergo the operation. Yet, she clung to the belief that this was a necessary step toward healing. Each small victory, a decrease in pain, increased mobility-became a celebration. With every passing day, she felt a renewed sense of hope, and the thought of returning to a life filled with joy and purpose began to feel tangible once more.

Through this arduous journey, Vanessa learned invaluable lessons about the strength of the human spirit and the importance of perseverance. While the Radvax therapy had initially brought her to an all-time low, it ultimately became a catalyst for her transformation. She discovered an inner reservoir of strength she never knew existed, one that pushed her to challenge the limitations imposed by her illness. Each setback became a stepping stone, teaching her that resilience is not merely about enduring pain but also about embracing the journey, no matter how difficult it may be. With newfound clarity, Vanessa began to redefine her understanding of what it meant to live fully.

As the weeks turned into months, Vanessa's body slowly began to heal. The initial agony gave way to a more manageable discomfort, and she found herself reclaiming small joys that she thought she had lost forever. Simple pleasures, like taking a walk outside or enjoying a warm cup of tea, took on new significance. The act of being present in those moments became a form of meditation, grounding her in the reality that life, despite its challenges, still held beauty and promise.

Empowered by her recovery, Vanessa decided to take an active role in her healing process. She researched nutrition and exercise, learning how to nourish her body in ways that would support its recovery. She began incorporating gentle yoga and meditation into her daily routine, seeking to harmonize her physical and emotional well-being. This holistic approach not only improved her physical strength but also provided her with a sense of control in a life that often felt chaotic. Each session on the mat became a celebration of her body's capabilities, a testament to her journey thus far.

In her quest for healing, Vanessa also sought to give back to others who were facing similar battles. She started volunteering at a local support group for individuals undergoing cancer treatments. Sharing her story and listening to the experiences of others created a sense of community that was deeply fulfilling. Vanessa found that in empowering others, she too felt empowered. The connections she forged provided her with a renewed sense of purpose, reinforcing her belief that even in the darkest times, there is light to be found in the shared human experience.

As she became more involved in the support group, Vanessa began to advocate for mental health awareness in conjunction with physical health. She realized that the emotional toll of illness was often overlooked, and she wanted to ensure that others felt heard and supported. She organized workshops that combined therapeutic practices with discussions about navigating the emotional landscape of illness. These gatherings became a safe space for individuals to express their fears, hopes, and triumphs, fostering a sense of camaraderie that was both healing and uplifting.

Vanessa's journey also led her to explore alternative therapies that complemented her medical treatment. She began working with a holistic practitioner who introduced her to acupuncture and herbal remedies. These modalities provided her with additional tools for managing pain and promoting overall well-being. While she remained committed to her medical treatments, she found solace in the idea that healing could come from multiple avenues, each contributing to her overall recovery.

As the anniversary of her diagnosis approached, Vanessa reflected on the profound changes she had undergone. She decided to commemorate the day not with sadness but with a celebration of life. She organized a gathering with family and friends, inviting them to share in her journey and acknowledge the strength it took to reach this point. The event was filled with laughter, tears, and heartfelt conversations, a tribute to the love and support that had propelled her forward. It was a reminder that while the path had been fraught with challenges, it had also been rich with connection and growth.

In the following months, Vanessa's health continued to improve, and she felt a renewed sense of vitality. With each passing day, she found herself more engaged in life, rediscovering passions that had been sidelined during her illness. She returned to painting, a hobby she had once cherished, allowing her creativity to flow freely once more. The act of expressing herself through art became a therapeutic outlet, a way to process her emotions and channel her experiences into something beautiful.

Amidst her recovery, Vanessa also began to think about the future. She contemplated her aspirations and dreams, once overshadowed by the weight of her condition. With a new perspective, she began to set goals for herself, both personally and professionally. She envisioned a life where she could help others navigate their own health challenges, perhaps by becoming a health coach or a motivational speaker. The idea of sharing her journey and the lessons learned filled her with excitement, fueling her desire to turn her struggles into strengths.

Vanessa's story became one of transformation, illustrating the power of resilience and the importance of community. Through her journey with Radvax therapy, she learned that while the road to recovery could be daunting, it was also filled with opportunities for growth and connection. The determination that had once kept her afloat became the foundation for a new chapter in her life, one where she could embrace both her past and her future with open arms. As she continued to heal, Vanessa looked toward the horizon with hope, ready to embrace whatever life had in store for her, armed with the knowledge that she was a survivor in every sense of the world.

Chapter Ten

Navigating the Medical Maze

Vanessa sat in the sterile room of her oncologist's office, her heart pounding as the doctor delivered the news that would change her life forever. Stage 4 kidney cancer. The words echoed in her mind, but it was the prognosis that struck her like a lightning bolt: only a month to live. As her world crumbled around her, she felt an overwhelming urge to fight, to navigate this medical maze that lay before her. She couldn't accept this fate without exploring every possible avenue, every potential treatment that could buy her more time.

The initial shock of the diagnosis left Vanessa feeling paralyzed. She had always been the one to care for others, a dedicated nurse who had spent years helping patients navigate their own health challenges. Now, she found herself on the other side of the stethoscope, grappling with her own mortality. As she left the office, she clutched the pamphlets the doctor had handed her, filled with information about clinical trials and palliative care options. It felt surreal, as if she were reading a script from someone else's life.

Determined to find a path forward, Vanessa immersed herself in research. Late into the night, she scoured the internet for information, reading medical journals and patient forums, trying to make sense of her diagnosis. Each article was a piece of a puzzle that seemed impossible to complete. She learned about immunotherapy, targeted treatments, and the importance of a healthy lifestyle. Every new piece of information fueled her resolve, igniting a flicker of hope amid the darkness that threatened to engulf her.

As days turned into a blur, Vanessa began reaching out to specialists across the country, seeking second opinions and alternative treatments. She found a community of fellow warriors who shared their stories of resilience and survival. With each conversation, she felt less isolated in her struggle. Vanessa learned about integrative approaches, combining conventional treatments with holistic care, nutrition, acupuncture, and mindfulness practices. She felt empowered by the prospect of taking an active role in her treatment, rather than merely being a passive recipient of care.

Her first appointment with a new oncologist was both terrifying and liberating. The new doctor's approach was refreshingly optimistic, emphasizing that survival rates were not set in stone and that many patients defied the odds. He presented her with a tailored treatment plan that included a combination of chemotherapy and experimental immunotherapy. Vanessa felt a surge of determination as she agreed to the plan, ready to embrace the fight with every ounce of strength she could muster.

However, the road ahead was fraught with challenges. Side effects from the chemotherapy began to take their toll, leaving her fatigued and nauseous. The initial spark of hope was often dimmed by the physical and emotional toll of the treatments. Vanessa found solace in journaling her experiences, documenting her feelings, and sharing her journey with friends and family. Each entry became a testament to her resilience, capturing the highs and lows of navigating a life-threatening illness.

In the midst of treatments, Vanessa also prioritized her mental health. She started attending a support group for cancer patients, where she connected with others who understood the unique struggles of living with a terminal diagnosis. Sharing her fears and triumphs in a safe space became a crucial part of her healing process. The stories of others inspired her and reminded her that she was not alone in this fight. Together, they found strength in vulnerability, creating bonds that transcended the fear of death.

As weeks slipped by, Vanessa discovered the power of gratitude. Despite the uncertainty of her future, she made a conscious effort to celebrate small victories, finishing a treatment cycle, enjoying a meal with loved ones, or spending a day in nature. Each moment of joy became a reminder that life, even in its fragility, was still beautiful. She learned to savor the present, focusing on what truly mattered: the love and support of her family and friends.

Vanessa also began exploring complementary therapies, such as yoga and meditation, which helped her manage stress and anxiety. These practices became vital tools in her arsenal, allowing her to cultivate a sense of peace amidst the chaos. She found solace in the rhythmic flow of yoga, using each pose as a metaphor for her journey, bending but never breaking, adapting to whatever came her way. Meditation offered her a refuge, a space to connect with her inner self and find clarity in the midst of uncertainty.

As her treatment progressed, Vanessa remained vigilant, attending regular check-ups and scans to monitor her condition. Each appointment was a mix of hope and dread, as she grappled with the fear of bad news. However, she was also met with moments of triumph. The scans showed promising results; the tumors had shrunk, and her prognosis had improved. With each milestone, she felt her resolve strengthen, bolstered by the knowledge that she was actively fighting against the odds.

Ultimately, Vanessa's journey through the medical maze of stage 4 kidney cancer taught her invaluable lessons about resilience, hope, and the importance of community. She realized that the fight against cancer was not just a battle waged in isolation but one that thrived in connection. Through her support group, she formed friendships that became lifelines. They shared laughter and tears, exchanged tips on managing side effects, and celebrated each other's milestones. This network of solidarity reminded her that she was part of something larger than herself, a collective of warriors who understood the weight of their shared experiences.

As Vanessa navigated the complexities of her treatment plan, she also began to advocate for herself more fiercely. No longer willing to accept anything less than the best possible care, she engaged in open discussions with her medical team about her options. She asked questions, sought clarifications, and expressed her preferences regarding her treatment. This newfound assertiveness empowered her, transforming her from a patient into an active participant in her healthcare journey. She learned that being informed was not just a privilege; it was a right that could significantly impact her quality of life.

With her health improving, Vanessa felt a surge of motivation to give back. Drawing from her experiences, she started a blog to document her journey, sharing insights, tips, and emotional truths about living with cancer. The blog quickly gained traction, attracting readers who resonated with her candid storytelling. Each post became a beacon of hope for others facing similar challenges, and the feedback she received reminded her of the healing power of vulnerability. Writing became a therapeutic outlet, allowing her to process her emotions while connecting with a wider community.

Inspired by her own journey, Vanessa also began volunteering at local hospitals, offering support to patients and their families. She found immense fulfillment in being a source of encouragement for those who felt lost and afraid. With her background as a nurse, she was uniquely equipped to provide both medical knowledge and emotional support. It was a way for her to reclaim her sense of purpose, transforming her experience of illness into a catalyst for compassion and connection.

As the months passed, Vanessa's health continued to improve, and her prognosis shifted dramatically. Her oncologist informed her that she had entered a state of remission, a term she had once thought was reserved for other people. The news was surreal, a culmination of her fierce determination, the support of her community, and the medical advancements that had fought alongside her. Yet, even with this victory, she remained grounded, knowing that the path ahead would still require vigilance and self-care.

Embracing her new lease on life, Vanessa made a conscious effort to prioritize her well-being. She adopted a holistic approach to health, focusing on nutrition, exercise, and mindfulness. The lessons learned during her treatment guided her decisions, reminding her to listen to her body and nurture her spirit. She discovered the joy of cooking, experimenting with plant-based recipes that not only nourished her body but also became a source of creativity and joy. Cooking together with friends became a cherished ritual, turning meals into celebrations rather than just sustenance.

The experience of living with cancer also ignited a passion for advocacy. Vanessa began speaking at cancer awareness events, sharing her story and raising awareness about kidney cancer and the importance of early detection. She collaborated with local organizations to promote educational initiatives, ensuring that others had access to vital information about symptoms and risk factors. By transforming her experience into a powerful message, she hoped to empower others to take charge of their health and advocate for themselves.

Through it all, Vanessa remained grateful for the lessons of resilience and hope. She understood that her journey was not just about surviving cancer; it was about truly living. She made a pact with herself to savor every moment, to find beauty in the mundane, and to cherish the connections that enriched her life. The fragility of existence became a source of inspiration, urging her to embrace vulnerability and authenticity in her relationships.

As the anniversary of her diagnosis approached, Vanessa planned a gathering with her loved ones. It was a celebration of life, resilience, and community. A reminder of how far she had come. Surrounded by friends and family, she shared her journey, the struggles, the victories, and the lessons learned. In that moment, she felt an overwhelming sense of gratitude for the support that had buoyed her during the darkest times. It was a testament to the power of love and connection, a celebration of the human spirit's capacity to navigate even the most daunting challenges.

Looking to the future, Vanessa felt a renewed sense of purpose. She had transformed her experience into a mission, one that centered on advocacy, support, and community. Inspired by her journey, she began to explore opportunities in healthcare policy, aiming to make a difference in the lives of others facing similar struggles. The journey through the medical maze had changed her profoundly, shaping her into a fierce advocate for herself and others. As she moved forward, she did so with hope in her heart, ready to embrace whatever lay ahead, armed with the knowledge that she was not alone in her fight.

Chapter Eleven

Moments of Doubt

Vanessa had always been a vibrant spirit, full of life and enthusiasm for the little things. She found joy in her morning rituals, the laughter of friends, and the warmth of family gatherings. However, when she received the diagnosis of stage 4 kidney cancer, that joy was suddenly eclipsed by an overwhelming sense of doubt and fear. Each day became a struggle, not only against the illness but also against the gnawing uncertainty that accompanied it. In those early days of diagnosis, Vanessa grappled with the question that haunted her thoughts: "Why me?"

As she sat in the sterile hospital room, draped in the uncomfortable gown, the weight of her situation pressed down on her. The oncologist's words echoed in her mind, and she replayed them over and over: "Stage 4." It felt like a finality, a judgment that she couldn't escape. Each time she looked in the mirror, she barely recognized herself. The vibrant woman she once was seemed to fade away, replaced by someone frail and vulnerable. Vanessa often found herself wondering if she would ever reclaim the life she had known, or if she would be forever marked by this diagnosis.

The doubts weren't just about her health; they seeped into her relationships as well. Vanessa worried about how her illness affected her loved ones. Would they see her as a burden? Would they grow weary of her struggles? In her mind, she envisioned them tiptoeing around her, avoiding conversations about the future, and it filled her with a profound sense of loneliness. She longed for connection, yet felt an overwhelming urge to shield them from her fears. The thought of being a source of pain for those she loved was almost unbearable.

As her treatment began, Vanessa faced the harsh realities of chemotherapy. The side effects were relentless and brutal, stripping away her energy and sense of normalcy. In moments of vulnerability, she found herself questioning the effectiveness of the treatment. Would it really help her, or was it just a way to prolong the inevitable? Doubts clouded her mind, and she often felt like a passenger in her own life, watching as the world moved on around her, while she remained stuck in a cycle of appointments, medications, and uncertainty.

Amidst the turmoil, moments of clarity emerged. Vanessa would occasionally find herself surrounded by friends who offered support and love unconditionally. These gatherings, though tinged with sadness, reminded her of the strength she still possessed. During these moments, she felt a flicker of hope, a belief that perhaps she could still navigate this journey. However, as soon as the laughter faded and the doors closed, doubt crept back in, whispering that the happiness was temporary, and the cancer loomed large on the horizon.

The emotional toll of her diagnosis became evident in Vanessa's daily life. Simple tasks, like going for a walk or cooking a meal, became monumental challenges. She often felt defeated, questioning her ability to cope with the physical and emotional demands of her condition. Doubts about her strength and resilience plagued her, making her wonder if she had the fortitude to fight this battle. Each step felt heavy, each breath a reminder of her fragility, and the darkness of despair threatened to engulf her.

Vanessa began to explore alternative therapies and holistic approaches, seeking solace in practices that promised healing. Yet, even these pursuits were tinged with doubt. Would they truly make a difference, or were they just distractions from the harsh reality of her situation? She oscillated between hope and skepticism, torn between the desire to take control of her health and the fear that she was grasping at straws. The uncertainty was exhausting, and she often wished for a clear answer, a definitive path that would lead her to recovery.

As the weeks passed, Vanessa found herself wrestling with the concept of acceptance. It was a struggle to embrace the reality of her diagnosis while still holding onto hope for recovery. She often questioned whether acceptance meant giving up or if it could be a way to find peace amidst the chaos. Her heart ached with the thought of surrendering to the illness, yet she knew that clinging to denial was equally unsustainable. This internal conflict left her feeling isolated, as if she were walking a tightrope between two worlds, one of hope and one of despair.

Vanessa's moments of doubt also extended to her future. The uncertainty of what lay ahead loomed large, often overshadowing her ability to enjoy the present. She found herself imagining different scenarios: a life cut short, milestones missed, and dreams unfulfilled. It was a heavy burden to carry, and at times, it felt insurmountable. The fear of the unknown became a constant companion, whispering that she might never experience the joys of life again. But in the quiet moments, she also found a determination to fight for those very experiences, even if it meant facing the darkness head-on.

Despite the doubts that plagued her, Vanessa found strength in the support network that had rallied around her. Friends and family became her lifeline, each one offering a unique form of encouragement. They brought flowers, cooked meals, and shared stories that made her laugh, reminding her that life still held moments of joy amidst the shadows. During these gatherings, she felt a sense of belonging that was hard to come by in the solitude of her hospital room. Yet, as the evening concluded and her loved ones departed, the silence would return, and with it, the familiar doubts would creep back in, leaving her to grapple with her thoughts in the stillness.

As days turned into weeks, Vanessa began to document her journey through journaling. Putting pen to paper became a therapeutic outlet, allowing her to express her fears, hopes, and moments of clarity. In writing, she confronted her doubts head-on, articulating the myriad of emotions that swirled within her. Each entry was a testament to her struggle, a raw reflection of her journey through cancer. This practice not only provided a release but also served as a reminder of her resilience; looking back at her entries, she often marveled at how far she had come, even in the face of uncertainty.

Yet, the moments of doubt persisted, especially when faced with the physical realities of her illness. Simple tasks like getting out of bed or taking a shower became Herculean efforts that left her drained. She often felt as though she were watching life pass her by from a distance, unable to participate fully. Each day brought a new wave of fatigue and discomfort, and with it, a familiar question: "Will I ever feel like myself again?" This internal dialogue became a constant source of anxiety, as she battled the physical manifestations of her cancer while simultaneously striving to maintain her spirit.

In seeking answers, Vanessa turned to support groups both online and in her community. It was there that she discovered a sense of camaraderie with others facing similar battles. They shared their stories, their fears, and their triumphs. Listening to their experiences brought her both comfort and more questions. While she found solace in their understanding, she also realized that each journey was unique, and the doubt began to creep in again. Would her path mirror theirs? Would she find the same strength they had? The fear of the unknown felt more palpable in these discussions, yet Vanessa also found herself inspired by the resilience of others.

One evening, as she sat in her living room, Vanessa decided to confront her doubts directly. She created a list of her fears and uncertainties, a tangible representation of the chaos in her mind. As she wrote, she began to understand that doubt was a natural part of her journey. It didn't define her; rather, it was a companion she would learn to navigate alongside. She acknowledged that it was okay to feel vulnerable and scared. In that moment of clarity, she realized that embracing her doubts could actually empower her, allowing her to approach her cancer journey with a mindset of acceptance rather than resistance.

Vanessa also began to explore mindfulness and meditation, desperate for moments of peace amidst the turmoil. These practices offered her a chance to disconnect from her anxieties and reconnect with her body. In those quiet moments, she learned to focus on her breath, embracing the present rather than getting lost in the "what-ifs." It was a small victory, but it became a cornerstone of her coping strategy. With each session, she learned to acknowledge her doubts without letting them consume her, cultivating a sense of calm that had previously felt elusive.

As her journey continued, Vanessa found herself developing a deeper appreciation for life's small moments. The sun filtering through the trees during a walk, the taste of her favorite meal, or the sound of laughter from her children became precious reminders of what she was fighting for. These moments sparked a flicker of hope in her heart, allowing her to push through the doubts. She realized that joy and sorrow could coexist, and even in the darkest times, there were glimmers of light that could guide her forward.

The turning point came when Vanessa met a woman who had recently celebrated her five-year cancer-free anniversary. This encounter ignited a spark of hope within her that she hadn't felt in a long time. Listening to the woman's story reminded Vanessa of the possibility of recovery, reigniting her desire to fight. She began to see her doubts not as barriers but as stepping stones on her journey. Inspired by this newfound perspective, she vowed to embrace each day with intention, to cherish her relationships, and to hold onto the belief that healing was possible.

In the end, Vanessa learned that doubt was a part of her journey, but it did not have to define her. It was a complex emotion, interwoven with her fears and hopes, but it was also a catalyst for growth. By confronting her doubts, she found strength in vulnerability and resilience in the face of adversity. As she continued her battle with stage 4 kidney cancer.

Vanessa began to redefine her relationship with doubt, viewing it as a natural component of her journey rather than an obstacle to overcome. This shift in perspective allowed her to cultivate a deeper understanding of herself. Instead of shying away from her fears, she started to engage with them, acknowledging their presence while refusing to let them dictate her actions. This newfound empowerment encouraged her to take proactive steps in her treatment and self-care. She became more vocal about her needs and desires, both in her medical care and her personal life, communicating openly with her doctors and loved ones.

The act of sharing her story with others became a source of strength for Vanessa. She started a article, documenting her experiences with cancer, the ups and downs, and the lessons she was learning along the way. Writing became a therapeutic outlet, allowing her to connect with others who were navigating similar challenges. The responses from her readers were overwhelmingly supportive, filled with encouragement and shared experiences. Through her words, Vanessa discovered that she wasn't alone in her journey; her vulnerability resonated with others and fostered a sense of community that uplifted her spirit.

As time went on, Vanessa also learned the importance of setting boundaries. She recognized that not every conversation needed to revolve around her illness, and it was okay to ask for moments of normalcy. She initiated activities that allowed her to escape the reality of cancer for a while. Movie nights, game evenings, and family outings. These moments of joy became a reminder of the life she was fighting for. By establishing a balance between acknowledging her illness and living fully, she found that doubt was less daunting when she surrounded herself with love and laughter.

Vanessa's journey through stage 4 kidney cancer taught her profound lessons about resilience, connection, and the multifaceted nature of hope. While moments of doubt would undoubtedly still arise, she now faced them with a sense of grace and acceptance. Her experience became a tapestry woven with strands of vulnerability and strength, of uncertainty and courage. Embracing the duality of her emotions allowed her to navigate her journey with a newfound purpose, understanding that every day was a gift to be cherished, no matter what challenges lay ahead. In the end, Vanessa resolved to live her life unapologetically, embracing the beauty of each moment while continuing to fight with all her heart.

Chapter Twelve

Finding Strength in Vulnerability

Vanessa had always been the epitome of strength in her community. Known for her unwavering resolve and fierce independence, she often found herself in the role of the caretaker, the problem-solver, the one who held everything together. However, deep inside, she struggled with the idea of vulnerability. The world had taught her that showing weakness was something to be avoided at all costs. But life, as it often does, presented her with challenges that forced her to reevaluate her understanding of strength.

One particularly challenging season began when Vanessa faced the loss of her beloved grandmother. The woman had been a source of wisdom and comfort, a guiding light in Vanessa's life. As she navigated through the grief, Vanessa felt an unfamiliar heaviness in her heart. She had always been the person others leaned on, but now she found herself in need of support. This was a turning point; she realized that she could no longer maintain her façade of invulnerability. The walls she had built around her heart started to crumble.

At first, allowing herself to feel the pain was terrifying. She had spent years suppressing her emotions, convinced that doing so was the hallmark of strength. But as the days passed, she found solace in the tears that flowed freely. Each tear was a release, a shedding of the weight she had carried for so long. It was through this process of grieving that Vanessa began to understand that vulnerability was not a sign of weakness but rather a testament to her humanity.

Seeking comfort, she confided in her closest friends, sharing her feelings of loss and sorrow. To her surprise, they welcomed her with open arms, offering support and understanding rather than judgment. In those moments of sharing, Vanessa discovered the power of connection. When she allowed herself to be vulnerable, she created a space for her friends to open up as well. They shared their own struggles, fears, and heartaches, which deepened their bonds and fostered an environment of mutual support.

Through this experience, Vanessa realized that vulnerability could be a strength, allowing for authentic relationships. It was a moment of epiphany when she recognized that everyone experiences pain, and it is through sharing these experiences that people grow closer. Her heart began to heal as she embraced the reality that it was okay to not be okay. She learned that vulnerability could lead to profound connections and that it was an essential part of the human experience.

As she continued to navigate her grief, Vanessa began to explore new ways of expressing herself. She joined a local art class, a space where she could create freely without the weight of expectations. The act of painting became a form of therapy, allowing her to channel her emotions onto the canvas. Each brushstroke was an exploration of her inner world, her pain, her joys, and her vulnerabilities. The art class became a sanctuary where vulnerability was celebrated, and she found strength in sharing her creations with others.

Embracing her vulnerability also led Vanessa to reevaluate her professional life. For years, she had pursued a career driven by ambition and the need to prove herself. After her grandmother's passing, however, she began to question what truly mattered to her. She realized that her career had often been a shield, a way to distract herself from her feelings. In recognizing this, she made the brave decision to shift her focus toward work that resonated with her heart, allowing her to connect with others in more meaningful ways.

In the months that followed, Vanessa became an advocate for mental health in her community. She began sharing her story, speaking openly about her journey through grief and the importance of vulnerability. The response was overwhelming; people began to reach out, sharing their own stories and struggles. Vanessa found herself in a new role, one that allowed her to empower others to embrace their vulnerabilities. She organized workshops and support groups, creating safe spaces where people could come together to share their experiences without fear of judgment.

The more she shared, the more Vanessa realized that vulnerability could be a profound source of strength. It was no longer something she viewed as a flaw but rather as a bridge that connected her to others. She discovered that when people were honest about their struggles, they inspired others to do the same, creating a ripple effect of healing within the community. Vanessa's authenticity resonated with many, and she felt a renewed sense of purpose as she created a movement centered on embracing vulnerability.

As time passed, Vanessa grew more comfortable with her new identity. She learned to celebrate her imperfections and recognize that vulnerability was an integral part of her journey. She embraced the idea that strength lies not in the absence of fear or pain, but in the courage to face them head-on. The lessons learned from her grandmother, combined with her own experiences, had shaped her into a person who could stand tall in her vulnerability, inspiring others to do the same.

Ultimately, Vanessa's journey of finding strength in vulnerability transformed her life. She became a beacon of hope for those around her, showing that it's okay to feel lost, to grieve, and to seek connection. Her story resonated far beyond her immediate circle; it reached individuals who had been silently battling their own demons, convincing themselves that they were alone in their struggles. Vanessa's willingness to share her pain opened the door for countless others to step into the light, embrace their vulnerabilities, and seek help. It was a powerful reminder that the human experience is intertwined, with each of our stories contributing to a larger tapestry of understanding and empathy.

As Vanessa continued to advocate for mental health awareness, she created a blog where she documented her journey. Each post was a reflection of her thoughts and feelings, a space where she could explore her vulnerabilities while encouraging others to do the same. The blog quickly gained traction, attracting readers from various backgrounds who found solace in her words. They shared their own stories in the comments, creating a vibrant community where vulnerability was not only accepted but celebrated. This online platform became a source of empowerment, proving that sharing one's struggles can lead to healing and resilience.

In her newfound role as a mental health advocate, Vanessa also collaborated with local organizations to host workshops focused on emotional well-being. These events provided tools and strategies for individuals to navigate their mental health journeys. The workshops emphasized the importance of vulnerability, teaching attendees that opening up about their feelings could foster deeper connections and provide much-needed support. Vanessa felt a profound sense of fulfillment in witnessing the transformative power of vulnerability in action, as participants began to share their stories, forming bonds that transcended their individual experiences.

Despite her growing success as an advocate, Vanessa faced moments of self-doubt. There were instances when she questioned whether her voice was truly making a difference. On particularly challenging days, she would return to her art as a means of self-reflection and expression. With each stroke of the brush, she poured her emotions onto the canvas, transforming her doubts into vibrant colors and powerful images. The act of creating became a therapeutic outlet, reminding her that her journey was valid and that her vulnerability was, in fact, a crucial part of her strength.

As Vanessa embraced her vulnerability more fully, she also sought to cultivate vulnerability in her personal relationships. She reached out to friends and family, initiating deeper conversations about their experiences, fears, and dreams. This openness transformed her relationships, fostering an environment where honesty and support flourished. Vanessa discovered that by sharing her own vulnerabilities, she encouraged those around her to do the same, creating a ripple effect of authenticity and connection that enriched her life and the lives of others.

Through her journey, Vanessa learned to celebrate her successes and acknowledge her struggles. She began to understand that vulnerability was not a destination but a continuous journey, one that required ongoing courage and self-compassion. Each time she faced a new challenge or experienced moments of doubt, she reminded herself of the strength she had found in her vulnerability. It became a guiding principle in her life, shaping her interactions and decisions as she moved forward with intention and purpose.

As the years went on, Vanessa's passion for mental health advocacy evolved into a mission to create lasting change in her community. She partnered with schools to implement programs focused on emotional intelligence and resilience, teaching young people the importance of embracing their vulnerabilities from an early age. Vanessa's vision was to cultivate a generation that understood that strength lies in authenticity, encouraging them to express their feelings rather than suppress them. This initiative became a labor of love, one that she poured her heart into, knowing that it could impact lives for years to come.

Ultimately, Vanessa's journey of finding strength in vulnerability not only transformed her own life but also created a ripple effect that touched countless others. She became a living testament to the idea that embracing one's true self, flaws, fears, and all, could lead to profound healing and connection. Vanessa had learned that vulnerability was not something to fear or hide away; it was a powerful tool for building relationships, fostering understanding, and inspiring change. With each step she took, she continued to shine a light on the beauty of vulnerability, encouraging others to join her on a path of authenticity, connection, and strength.

Chapter Thirteen

The Power of Positivity

Positivity is often viewed as a mere attitude, a cheerful demeanor in the face of challenges. However, it is so much more than that. It serves as a powerful catalyst for change, an essential ingredient in the recipe for resilience. The power of positivity can be transformative, impacting not only the individual harboring it but also those around them. When faced with adversity, a positive outlook can inspire hope, foster connections, and create pathways to solutions that may have seemed impossible otherwise.

Vanessa is a shining example of this transformative power. Throughout her life, she has encountered numerous obstacles—personal losses, health challenges, and professional setbacks. Yet, instead of succumbing to despair, Vanessa has embraced a positive mindset, using it as her shield against the storms of life. Her journey is a testament to the strength that positivity can cultivate, enabling her to endure hardships that would have overwhelmed many.

From a young age, Vanessa learned the importance of resilience. Growing up in a challenging environment, she was often faced with circumstances that tested her limits. However, she quickly discovered that maintaining a positive attitude was her greatest asset. Through her experiences, she developed a mantra. "Every challenge is an opportunity for growth." This belief became the cornerstone of her outlook, allowing her to navigate the tumultuous waters of life with grace and determination.

One of the most profound aspects of Vanessa's strength lies in her ability to reframe situations. When confronted with setbacks, she doesn't dwell on what went wrong. Instead, she focuses on what she can learn from the experience. This perspective not only helps her to cope but also empowers her to take proactive steps toward improvement. By viewing challenges as opportunities, Vanessa cultivates a mindset that encourages innovation and creativity, propelling her forward even in the darkest times.

The ripple effect of Vanessa's positivity extends beyond her personal journey. Friends, family, and even acquaintances have been inspired by her unwavering spirit. In group settings, her infectious enthusiasm often uplifts others, creating an environment where collaboration and support thrive. Vanessa has a unique ability to remind those around her of their own strengths, encouraging them to tap into their inner reservoirs of resilience. Her presence serves as a beacon of hope, illustrating the profound impact one individual can have on an entire community.

Moreover, Vanessa's journey highlights the importance of self-care in maintaining a positive outlook. She understands that nurturing her physical, emotional, and mental well-being is crucial for her endurance. By prioritizing activities that bring her joy, such as yoga, meditation, and spending time in nature, Vanessa replenishes her energy and fortifies her spirit. This commitment to self-care not only sustains her positivity but also equips her to support others effectively.

In times of adversity, Vanessa often turns to gratitude as a powerful tool for maintaining her positive mindset. She practices daily gratitude, taking moments to reflect on the blessings in her life, no matter how small. This practice has taught her to appreciate the silver linings, even in the most challenging situations. By focusing on what she has rather than what she lacks, Vanessa cultivates a sense of abundance that fuels her resilience and empowers her to keep moving forward.

The power of community cannot be understated in Vanessa's journey. She recognizes that positivity thrives in an environment of support and connection. By surrounding herself with like-minded individuals who share her values, she creates a network of encouragement that bolsters her strength. Together, they celebrate each other's victories and provide comfort during tough times, reinforcing the idea that no one has to face their struggles alone.

Vanessa's story is a powerful reminder that positivity is not about ignoring challenges or wearing rose-colored glasses. It is about acknowledging reality while choosing to focus on possibilities. Her strength to endure stems from her decision to confront adversity with courage and optimism. This approach not only enhances her own life but also serves as a guiding light for others seeking to navigate their own battles.

In conclusion, the power of positivity is a force that can transform lives, and Vanessa embodies this truth. Through her unwavering spirit, she demonstrates that resilience is not just about enduring hardships but also about thriving in the face of them. Her journey is a celebration of the human spirit's capacity to rise above adversity, reminding us all that with a positive mindset and a strong support system, we can overcome even the most daunting challenges. Vanessa's strength serves as an inspiration, urging us to harness the power of positivity in our own lives and embrace the transformative journey it offers.

While positivity is often associated with strength, it is essential to recognize that it does not negate the experience of vulnerability. Vanessa has learned that embracing vulnerability is a sign of true courage. By allowing herself to feel and express her emotions, she creates a more authentic connection with herself and others. This openness fosters deeper relationships, as those around her feel safe to share their struggles and triumphs. Vanessa's willingness to be vulnerable not only enhances her own resilience but also cultivates an environment where positivity can thrive.

In moments of hardship, Vanessa often reflects on her past experiences to draw strength. She keeps a journal filled with memories of overcoming obstacles, reminding herself of the challenges she has faced and conquered. These reflections serve as a powerful reminder that she has the capacity to endure and emerge stronger. By documenting her journey, she also creates a legacy of resilience that can inspire others who may find themselves in similar situations, reinforcing the notion that they, too, can rise above their challenges.

Moreover, Vanessa has found that sharing her story amplifies the power of positivity. By openly discussing her experiences with adversity in various forums, whether through public speaking, writing, or informal conversations. She creates a ripple effect of encouragement. Her vulnerability resonates with others, allowing them to see that they are not alone in their struggles. As she shares her journey, Vanessa empowers others to recognize their strengths, inspiring them to adopt a positive mindset in the face of their own challenges.

Vanessa's approach to positivity also includes a commitment to lifelong learning. She believes that every experience, whether good or bad, offers valuable lessons. By maintaining a curious mindset, she embraces opportunities to learn from others and expand her knowledge. This thirst for growth not only enriches her own life but also equips her with the tools necessary to navigate future challenges. For Vanessa, the journey of self-improvement is ongoing, and she approaches it with enthusiasm and optimism.

In her professional life, Vanessa's positivity has become a cornerstone of her leadership style. As a manager, she fosters a culture of positivity within her team, encouraging collaboration, creativity, and open communication. She understands that a positive work environment leads to increased productivity and innovation. By acknowledging her team's efforts and celebrating their successes, Vanessa builds a strong sense of community that motivates everyone to strive for excellence. Her leadership is a testament to the idea that positivity can drive not only individual success but also collective achievement.

Vanessa also places great importance on mindfulness as a practice that enhances her positivity. By incorporating mindfulness techniques into her daily routine, such as meditation and deep breathing exercises, she cultivates a sense of inner peace and clarity. This practice allows her to remain grounded, even in the face of stress and uncertainty. Mindfulness helps Vanessa to respond to challenges with intention rather than reacting impulsively, reinforcing her ability to maintain a positive outlook amid chaos.

The power of positivity extends to Vanessa's relationships, where she actively seeks to uplift those around her. She believes that a supportive network is vital for resilience. By being a source of encouragement for her friends and family, Vanessa creates a ripple effect of positivity that reverberates throughout her community. Whether it's through a kind word, a listening ear, or thoughtful gestures, she invests in the well-being of others, fostering a culture of support that ultimately strengthens her own resilience.

In her quest for positivity, Vanessa also recognizes the importance of setting boundaries. She understands that while it is essential to be a source of support for others, she must also protect her own energy and mental health. By establishing healthy boundaries, Vanessa ensures that she can remain a positive force without feeling overwhelmed. This self-awareness empowers her to engage with others authentically while preserving her own well-being.

As Vanessa continues her journey, she envisions a future where positivity is not just an individual choice but a collective movement. She dreams of a world where people support one another in fostering resilience, where challenges are viewed as opportunities for growth rather than insurmountable obstacles. Through her actions and advocacy, Vanessa aims to contribute to this vision, believing that together, we can create a brighter, more positive future.

Ultimately, Vanessa's story serves as a reminder that the power of positivity is a choice we can all make. It is not a denial of reality but an active engagement with it. An assertion that we can face our struggles with hope and determination. By embracing positivity, vulnerability, and resilience, we can navigate life's challenges with grace. Vanessa's journey encourages us to harness our inner strength and inspire those around us, creating a ripple effect of positivity that can change lives and communities for the better. In a world where negativity often dominates, Vanessa stands as a beacon of hope, reminding us of the incredible potential we all hold within ourselves to rise, endure, and thrive.

Chapter Fourteen

Facing Fear, Vanessa's Journey Through Her First Surgery.

Facing fear is often one of life's greatest challenges, and for Vanessa, her first surgery was a pivotal moment that tested her courage and resilience. The days leading up to the surgery were filled with a whirlwind of emotions, anxiety, uncertainty, and a profound sense of vulnerability. Vanessa had never undergone a surgical procedure before, and the prospect of being placed under anesthesia and having her body operated on filled her with trepidation. Yet, she was determined to confront her fears head-on, believing that acknowledging and facing them was the first step toward overcoming them.

In the weeks prior to the surgery, Vanessa took time to educate herself about the procedure. She met with her surgeon, asked questions, and sought clarity on what to expect. This proactive approach helped her feel more in control of the situation. Vanessa understood that knowledge could be a powerful antidote to fear; by familiarizing herself with the process, she was able to demystify the experience. Each conversation with her medical team chipped away at the anxiety that loomed over her, replacing it with a sense of empowerment.

However, no amount of preparation could eliminate all of Vanessa's fears. The night before her surgery was particularly challenging. As she lay in bed, her mind raced with "what if" scenarios, contemplating everything from the surgery's risks to the possibility of complications. In those moments of vulnerability, she found herself grappling with the fear of the unknown. It was a stark reminder that fear is often rooted in uncertainty, and that facing it requires confronting deeply held beliefs about safety and control.

To manage her anxiety, Vanessa turned to her trusted coping mechanisms. She practiced deep breathing exercises, which helped to ground her and calm her racing heart. Additionally, she engaged in positive affirmations, repeating phrases like "I am strong" and "I will get through this" to herself. These practices served as a reminder of her inner strength and resilience, reinforcing her belief that she could navigate this challenging experience with grace.

The morning of the surgery arrived, and Vanessa felt a mix of emotions. As she prepared to leave for the hospital, she took a moment to reflect on her journey thus far. This was not just a physical procedure; it was a significant step toward reclaiming her health and well-being. With each step she took, she reminded herself that this surgery was an opportunity for healing, not just a source of fear. Embracing this perspective helped to shift her mindset, allowing her to focus on the positive outcome she hoped to achieve.

Upon arriving at the hospital, Vanessa was greeted by a warm and supportive medical staff. Their compassion and professionalism put her at ease, reminding her that she was not alone in this journey. As she was led to the pre-operative area, she engaged in light conversation with the nurses, finding comfort in their presence. This human connection reminded her that fear could be mitigated by the kindness and support of others, and that she was surrounded by a team dedicated to her care.

As Vanessa was wheeled into the operating room, she felt a surge of emotions, fear, hope, and determination intertwined within her. The bright lights and sterile environment were intimidating, but she took a deep breath and focused on her intention, to emerge from the surgery healthier and stronger. In that moment, she realized that facing her fears was not just about overcoming them; it was also about embracing the journey of healing. With this newfound perspective, she felt a sense of calm wash over her as the anesthesiologist prepared her for the procedure.

As she drifted into unconsciousness, Vanessa felt a mix of relief and gratitude. She had faced her fears and taken a courageous step toward healing. In that vulnerable moment, she surrendered to the process, trusting in the expertise of her medical team and the strength of her own spirit. This act of surrender was a powerful statement of resilience, a testament to her ability to confront her fears and move forward despite uncertainty.

When Vanessa awoke after the surgery, she was met with a wave of relief. The procedure had gone well, and she felt a sense of accomplishment wash over her. In the days that followed, she experienced physical discomfort, but she also felt a deep sense of pride in having faced her fears head-on. Each moment of recovery reminded her of her strength and the importance of resilience in the face of adversity. She realized that her journey was far from over, but the first step had been taken, and she was ready to embrace the healing process.

Throughout her recovery, Vanessa reflected on the lessons learned during her surgical experience. She recognized that fear, while natural, should not dictate her choices or hinder her progress. Instead, she vowed to use her experience as a source of inspiration for herself and others. By sharing her story of facing fear, she hoped to empower those who might be grappling with similar challenges, reminding them that courage is not the absence of fear but rather the ability to move forward in spite of it.

As Vanessa navigated her recovery, she also discovered the power of community. Friends and family rallied around her, offering support in countless ways, from preparing meals to simply being present for her. This outpouring of love reminded her that vulnerability can be a bridge to connection rather than a barrier. Each visit from a loved one provided an opportunity for meaningful conversations and laughter, reinforcing the idea that sharing her struggles not only lightened her burden but also invited others to share their own experiences of fear and resilience.

One afternoon, while sitting on her couch with a friend, Vanessa opened up about her surgical fears. She spoke candidly about the anxiety she felt leading up to the procedure and the moments of doubt that crept in. Her friend, in turn, shared her own story of facing a similar fear during a significant life event. This exchange left Vanessa feeling understood and validated. It was a poignant reminder that everyone faces challenges, and by sharing those challenges, they can find solace in one another's experiences.

In the weeks following her surgery, Vanessa made it a priority to document her recovery journey in her journal. Writing became a therapeutic outlet, allowing her to express her thoughts and emotions freely. She recorded her triumphs, no matter how small, as well as the moments of frustration that reminded her healing takes time. This practice not only helped her process her experience but also served as a testament to her growth. As she flipped through the pages, she could see how far she had come, transforming fear into empowerment, vulnerability into strength.

Inspired by her experience, Vanessa decided to channel her newfound perspective into a project aimed at helping others facing medical fears. She began organizing workshops and support groups where individuals could come together to share their stories and strategies for coping with anxiety related to surgery and health. These gatherings quickly became a source of inspiration and encouragement, creating a safe space for participants to express their fears without judgment. Vanessa found immense joy in facilitating these discussions, knowing that she was contributing to a community of support and hope.

Through these workshops, Vanessa also learned the importance of self-compassion. She realized that it was okay to feel fear and anxiety; these emotions did not diminish her strength. Instead of pushing her feelings aside, she embraced them as part of her healing process. By allowing herself to experience and acknowledge her emotions, she was better equipped to manage them. This newfound self-compassion extended beyond her surgical journey and became a guiding principle in her life moving forward.

As Vanessa continued her healing journey, she began to practice mindfulness regularly. She discovered that mindfulness techniques, such as meditation and yoga, helped her stay grounded and present, especially during moments of anxiety. By focusing on her breath and the sensations in her body, she learned to cultivate a sense of calm within herself. This practice became a powerful tool in her arsenal, enabling her to navigate life's uncertainties with greater ease and confidence.

With each passing day, Vanessa not only healed physically but also grew emotionally and spiritually. She became more attuned to her body and its needs, developing a deeper appreciation for her health and well-being. This newfound awareness allowed her to approach life with gratitude rather than fear. Instead of viewing challenges as insurmountable obstacles, she began to see them as opportunities for growth and self-discovery.

The experience of facing her fears during her first surgery ultimately transformed Vanessa's outlook on life. She emerged from the ordeal with a profound understanding of her own resilience and a commitment to living authentically. Armed with the lessons she had learned, she felt empowered to tackle future challenges head-on, knowing that fear didn't have to dictate her path. Instead, she embraced the idea that every fear conquered was a step toward personal growth and greater self-awareness.

In sharing her journey with others, Vanessa hoped to inspire those who struggled with fear, reminding them that they are not alone. Through her workshops and written reflections, she aimed to create a culture of openness, where vulnerability was celebrated and stories of courage were shared. By fostering connections rooted in shared experiences, Vanessa believed that individuals could find strength in community and encouragement in one another's journeys, ultimately transforming fear into empowerment and hope.

Chapter Fifteen

The Road To Recovery

Vanessa had always been a vibrant individual, known for her infectious laughter and unwavering spirit. However, everything changed when she received the shocking diagnosis of kidney cancer. It was a moment that felt surreal, leaving her grappling with a whirlwind of emotions, confusion, fear, and uncertainty about the future. Vanessa had always been the pillar of strength for her family, and now she found herself facing a battle that would test her resilience in ways she never imagined.

After the initial diagnosis, Vanessa's world became a blur of medical appointments and consultations. She met with oncologists who explained the various treatment options available to her. The thought of chemotherapy, surgery, and the unknown effects of each weighed heavily on her mind. Vanessa took her time to process the information, determined to make informed decisions about her treatment while also seeking a second opinion to ensure she was on the right path. This proactive approach helped her regain a sense of control in a situation that felt overwhelmingly chaotic.

Once her treatment plan was finalized, Vanessa prepared herself mentally and physically for the journey ahead. She adopted a healthier lifestyle, incorporating a balanced diet and regular exercise into her routine to bolster her immune system. This newfound dedication to her health not only improved her physical well-being but also provided her with a sense of purpose. She began journaling her thoughts and experiences, documenting her journey to recovery and finding solace in her writing as a therapeutic outlet.

As Vanessa began her first round of chemotherapy, she was met with a range of side effects that tested her resolve. Fatigue, nausea, and hair loss became unwelcome companions in her daily life, but she refused to let them define her experience. Drawing strength from her support network of family and friends, she found comfort in their encouragement. They became her cheerleaders, reminding her of the resilient woman she had always been, and helping her navigate the emotional rollercoaster that accompanied her treatment.

During this challenging time, Vanessa discovered a newfound appreciation for the small moments in life. She found joy in simple pleasures, such as reading her favorite books, watching the sunset, and spending quality time with loved ones. Each day became an opportunity for gratitude, as she learned to celebrate the small victories along her road to recovery. With each passing week, she felt more empowered, realizing that her spirit was stronger than the cancer that sought to bring her down.

As Vanessa continued her treatment, she also sought out support groups for cancer patients. Connecting with others who were on similar journeys provided her with invaluable insight and camaraderie. Sharing her fears and triumphs with those who truly understood her struggles helped to alleviate some of the emotional burdens she carried. Their stories inspired her, fostering a sense of hope that propelled her forward, even on the darkest days when doubt crept in.

After months of treatment, the day finally arrived for Vanessa's follow-up scans. Anxiety filled the air as she awaited the results, but she reminded herself of the strength she had cultivated throughout her journey. When the doctor delivered the news that her cancer was in remission, an overwhelming wave of relief washed over her. Tears of joy flowed freely as she embraced her family, grateful for the love and support that had carried her through the darkest of times.

In the aftermath of her diagnosis, Vanessa made it her mission to raise awareness about kidney cancer. She began volunteering with local organizations and sharing her story to inspire others facing similar battles. Her journey had taught her the importance of early detection and the power of community support. By becoming an advocate, Vanessa not only found purpose in her experience but also empowered others to take charge of their health.

As she continued to heal, Vanessa focused on self-care, both physically and emotionally. She explored mindfulness practices, such as yoga and meditation, which helped her cultivate a sense of inner peace. These practices became essential tools in her recovery, allowing her to manage stress and maintain a positive outlook. Vanessa learned to listen to her body and prioritize her well-being, understanding that recovery was not just about physical health but emotional resilience as well.

Today, Vanessa stands as a testament to the strength of the human spirit. Her journey through kidney cancer has transformed her perspective on life, leading her to appreciate every moment and cherish her relationships. She became a beacon of hope for those around her, reminding everyone that while the road to recovery may be fraught with challenges, it is also filled with opportunities for growth, connection, and healing. With each passing day, she embraces her new chapter, determined to live life to the fullest and inspire others along the way.

In sharing her story, Vanessa hopes to encourage those facing similar struggles to never lose hope. She believes that every challenge can lead to a greater understanding of oneself, and that even in the darkest moments, there is light to be found. Vanessa's journey serves as a reminder that resilience, love, and community can guide us through the most difficult of times, leading to a brighter and more fulfilling future.

Vanessa's journey through kidney cancer was not just a battle against a formidable illness; it was a testament to her unyielding spirit and determination. From the moment she received her diagnosis, she made a conscious decision to fight. The initial shock of the news was overwhelming, but instead of succumbing to despair, she resolved to take an active role in her recovery. This mindset became her anchor, guiding her through the turbulent waters of treatment and uncertainty. Vanessa understood that her attitude would play a crucial role in her journey, and she refused to let cancer define her.

Throughout her treatment, Vanessa faced numerous challenges that tested her resolve. Chemotherapy brought about debilitating side effects, including fatigue and nausea, but she approached each day with a fierce determination to overcome. Rather than allowing these obstacles to deter her, she sought ways to manage them. Vanessa educated herself about the side effects and discovered techniques to alleviate them, such as dietary adjustments and alternative therapies. This proactive approach not only empowered her but also reinforced her belief that she was an active participant in her healing process.

One of the most significant factors in Vanessa's recovery was her unwavering support system. She surrounded herself with family and friends who encouraged her every step of the way. Their unwavering belief in her strength bolstered her own confidence and served as a constant reminder that she was not alone in her fight. Vanessa often reflected on the power of their support, recognizing that it fueled her determination to persevere. She cherished the moments spent with loved ones, which provided her with the emotional nourishment needed to face her treatment head-on.

As part of her journey, Vanessa also learned the importance of self-compassion. She recognized that it was okay to have moments of vulnerability and doubt. Embracing her feelings allowed her to process her emotions fully, rather than suppressing them. Journaling became a vital outlet for her, where she could express her fears, hopes, and triumphs. By confronting her emotions honestly, she found clarity and strength, reinforcing her commitment to recovery. This practice of self-reflection became a cornerstone of her resilience, reminding her of the progress she was making.

In addition to emotional support, Vanessa prioritized her physical health. She adopted a holistic approach to her recovery, incorporating nutritious foods, regular exercise, and mindfulness practices into her daily routine. As she made healthier choices, she noticed improvements in her energy levels and overall well-being. This positive feedback loop motivated her to maintain her commitment to her health. Each workout, each nourishing meal, felt like a small victory, reinforcing her belief that she was taking control of her recovery.

Vanessa's determination also led her to seek knowledge about kidney cancer and its treatment options. She spent countless hours researching, attending workshops, and connecting with medical professionals. This thirst for knowledge empowered her to ask questions and advocate for herself during consultations. By arming herself with information, she was able to approach her treatment with confidence and clarity. Vanessa realized that understanding her condition was not only empowering but also essential for making informed decisions about her care.

As the months passed, Vanessa's perseverance began to yield positive results. After undergoing surgery and several rounds of chemotherapy, she received the news she had been hoping for: her cancer was in remission. The moment felt surreal, but deep down, she knew that her unwavering belief in herself had played a significant role in this outcome. She embraced this victory not just as a personal achievement but as a testament to the power of resilience and self-belief. This pivotal moment solidified her understanding that recovery is a journey, one that requires both tenacity and hope.

In the aftermath of her diagnosis and treatment, Vanessa felt a renewed sense of purpose. She became an advocate for cancer awareness, sharing her story to inspire others facing similar battles. Through public speaking engagements and community outreach, she emphasized the importance of self-advocacy and the impact of a positive mindset. Vanessa wanted others to know that the road to recovery might be challenging, but it is navigable with determination and support. Her story became a beacon of hope for many, illustrating that perseverance can lead to remarkable outcomes.

Vanessa also discovered the power of gratitude throughout her journey. She made it a daily practice to reflect on the things she was thankful for, no matter how small. This shift in focus helped her cultivate a positive outlook, even on the toughest days. By regularly acknowledging her blessings, she found strength in the face of adversity. Gratitude became a crucial element of her recovery, reminding her of the beauty that still existed in her life amid challenges.

Today, Vanessa stands as a symbol of resilience and strength. Her journey through kidney cancer has transformed her perspective on life, instilling in her a profound appreciation for every moment. She continues to embrace each day with enthusiasm, never taking her health for granted. Vanessa's experience has taught her that success is not solely defined by the absence of illness but by the courage to confront challenges head-on and the determination to thrive despite them.

Chapter Sixteen

Embracing The Journey

Vanessa had always been known for her vibrant spirit and unwavering determination. When she was diagnosed with kidney cancer, the news felt like a thunderbolt striking her seemingly perfect life. It was a shock that rattled her to the core, but it also ignited a fire within her. Instead of letting fear and despair consume her, Vanessa chose to embrace the journey ahead. She understood that this was not just a battle against illness but an opportunity for growth, self-discovery, and connection.

In the early days following her diagnosis, Vanessa immersed herself in research about kidney cancer. She read medical journals, joined support groups, and spoke with specialists. This new knowledge empowered her, transforming her fear into a sense of control. Vanessa realized that understanding her condition was crucial not only for her treatment but also for her mental and emotional well-being. She began documenting her journey, keeping a journal where she poured out her thoughts, fears, and hopes. Writing became a therapeutic outlet, allowing her to confront her emotions head-on.

As she underwent treatment, Vanessa faced physical challenges that tested her resilience. The side effects of chemotherapy were daunting, leaving her fatigued and vulnerable. Yet, in those moments of weakness, she found strength in her support network. Friends and family rallied around her, offering encouragement and assistance. Vanessa learned the importance of vulnerability; asking for help was not a sign of weakness but an act of courage. These connections enriched her journey, reminding her that she was never alone in her fight.

One day, while sitting in the hospital waiting room, Vanessa met another patient named Maria. They struck up a conversation that quickly blossomed into a deep friendship. Maria shared her own cancer journey, filled with struggles and triumphs, and Vanessa found solace in their shared experiences. They became each other's cheerleaders, celebrating small victories and providing comfort during setbacks. This bond illuminated the fact that every journey is unique, yet there are universal threads of hope and resilience that connect them all.

As treatment progressed, Vanessa began to shift her focus from the disease itself to the life she wanted to live moving forward. She started to explore mindfulness practices, such as meditation and yoga, which helped her cultivate a sense of peace amidst the chaos. These practices became essential tools in her healing journey, allowing her to reconnect with her body and mind. Vanessa learned to appreciate the small moments, the warmth of the sun on her face, the laughter of friends, the taste of her favorite foods. Each day became an opportunity to find joy, even in the face of adversity.

Vanessa's journey also inspired her to give back to the community. She began volunteering at local cancer support organizations, sharing her story and lending her voice to those who felt unheard. She organized workshops and support groups, fostering a sense of community and belonging among patients. This act of service not only helped others but also reinforced her own healing. Vanessa realized that by helping others, she was also helping herself; it was a beautiful cycle of compassion and strength.

As the months passed, Vanessa's perspective on life continued to evolve. She became more attuned to her values, prioritizing what truly mattered. Relationships deepened, and superficial concerns faded away. She embraced spontaneity, seeking adventures that filled her heart with joy. Whether it was a weekend getaway or simply trying a new recipe at home, each experience became a testament to her resilience and zest for life. Vanessa learned that living fully was not about avoiding challenges but about facing them with courage and grace.

The day finally came when Vanessa received the news she had been waiting for, her cancer was in remission. The relief washed over her like a tidal wave, but she quickly realized that her journey was far from over. Remission was a new chapter, one that required ongoing self-care and vigilance. Vanessa embraced this reality with open arms, grateful for the lessons learned and the strength gained. She understood that her experience with kidney cancer had transformed her in ways she could never have imagined.

With her newfound perspective, Vanessa became an advocate for cancer awareness and early detection. She spoke at conferences, sharing her story to inspire others to take charge of their health. Vanessa encouraged people to listen to their bodies and seek medical advice when something felt off. Her mission was clear: to empower others to embrace their journeys, whatever they might be. She found purpose in her advocacy, knowing that her voice could make a difference in the lives of those facing similar battles.

Through it all, Vanessa remained grateful for the support she had received. She often reflected on the power of community during her darkest hours. Her journey had taught her the importance of connection, love, and vulnerability. She became an active participant in her own life, choosing to celebrate every milestone, no matter how small. Vanessa's journey through kidney cancer was not just about survival; it was a testament to the human spirit's ability to thrive amidst adversity.

As she looked toward the future, Vanessa felt a renewed sense of hope and determination. She had transformed her experience into a powerful narrative of resilience and empowerment. With each passing day, she embraced her identity not merely as a cancer survivor but as a warrior who had faced the storm and emerged stronger. Vanessa understood that her journey would continue to shape her life in profound ways. She had developed a deeper appreciation for her own strength, as well as a commitment to living authentically.

The lessons Vanessa learned throughout her cancer journey extended beyond her own experience. She felt a responsibility to share her story with others, to remind them that it's okay to feel vulnerable and to ask for help. She began to host workshops that focused on emotional well-being, inviting people to explore their fears and feelings about illness and health. By creating a safe space for dialogue, Vanessa fostered healing not only for herself but for those who attended. She found that sharing her story allowed others to share theirs, creating a ripple effect of hope and understanding.

In her advocacy work, Vanessa also emphasized the importance of mental health. She had experienced firsthand how the psychological toll of illness could weigh heavily on a person. She collaborated with mental health professionals to develop resources aimed at supporting cancer patients in managing stress and anxiety. Vanessa's workshops often included mindfulness exercises and coping strategies, which she found invaluable during her own treatment. By integrating mental health into the conversation about cancer, she aimed to normalize the emotional struggles that accompany physical illness.

As Vanessa continued her advocacy, she also sought to give back to the medical professionals who had supported her during her treatment. She organized appreciation events for nurses and doctors, recognizing their tireless efforts and compassion. Vanessa wanted them to know how much their work meant to patients like herself. In turn, this created a stronger bond between the medical community and survivors, fostering an environment of mutual respect and understanding. The appreciation events became a celebration of life, emphasizing the collaborative efforts required in the fight against cancer.

One of the most significant changes Vanessa experienced was her newfound perspective on time and priorities. She began to live with intention, making choices that aligned with her values. This meant spending more quality time with loved ones, pursuing her passions, and finding joy in everyday moments. She often took spontaneous trips to the beach or embarked on hikes in nature, recognizing that these experiences were vital for her well-being. Vanessa's laughter became contagious, and her zest for life inspired those around her to embrace their own journeys, however uncertain they may be.

Reflecting on her journey, Vanessa was grateful for the challenges she had faced. They had shaped her into the person she was today, a person who understood the fragility of life yet remained unyielding in her pursuit of happiness and fulfillment. She had discovered that life was not just about the hurdles but also about the connections forged along the way. Vanessa found beauty in her scars and recognized that they told a story of resilience, strength, and hope.

As she looked to the future, Vanessa felt a sense of peace wash over her. She knew that her journey through kidney cancer had transformed her life in ways she could never have anticipated. With each step forward, she was committed to living authentically, embracing challenges, and inspiring others to do the same. Vanessa had emerged from the shadows of illness, not just as a survivor but as a beacon of hope, ready to illuminate the path for others navigating their own journeys. Her story was a reminder that, even in the face of adversity, there is always an opportunity for growth, connection, and renewal.

Chapter Seventeen

Vanessa's Radvax Therapy Chronicles

Vanessa had always been fascinated by the intersection of science and human experience. Her journey into the world of Radvax therapy began when she was diagnosed with a rare autoimmune disorder that left her feeling trapped in her own body. Traditional treatments provided only temporary relief, and the side effects often felt more daunting than the disease itself. It was during a particularly challenging phase of her illness that she stumbled upon Radvax therapy, a relatively new and innovative approach designed to stimulate the body's immune response without the harsh side effects of conventional medications.

The first step in Vanessa's Radvax therapy journey was an extensive consultation with Dr. Simmons, a leading immunologist who specialized in this groundbreaking treatment. He explained how Radvax therapy worked by leveraging the body's own immune system to combat the anomalies causing her autoimmune disorder. "It's like giving your immune system a gentle nudge," he said, his eyes gleaming with enthusiasm. Vanessa was intrigued but cautious; she had heard many promises from the medical community before. However, the possibility of regaining control over her body was too enticing to ignore.

Once she decided to proceed with the therapy, Vanessa was enrolled in a clinical trial that aimed to gather more data on Radvax's efficacy and safety. The first few weeks were filled with a mixture of hope and anxiety. Each session consisted of targeted injections designed to prime her immune system. Vanessa meticulously documented her experiences in a journal, noting every change in her symptoms, energy levels, and emotional state. It became a therapeutic outlet, helping her process the highs and lows of her treatment.

As the weeks turned into months, Vanessa began to notice subtle changes. The fatigue that had previously enveloped her like a fog began to lift, and her chronic pain eased. While she was careful not to celebrate too soon, she felt a renewed sense of optimism. Alongside her physical symptoms, Vanessa noticed a shift in her mental outlook. The therapy was not just altering her body; it was also transforming her perspective on illness and healing. She started to see herself not just as a patient but as an active participant in her own recovery.

Vanessa's journey through Radvax therapy was not without its challenges. There were days when she felt overwhelmed by the enormity of her condition, and the emotional toll of chronic illness weighed heavily on her. However, she found solace in her growing community of fellow patients, many of whom were also undergoing Radvax therapy. They formed a support network, sharing their stories, fears, and triumphs. Through their shared experiences, Vanessa discovered the power of connection and the importance of having a tribe to lean on during tough times.

As her therapy progressed, Vanessa became increasingly engaged in advocacy work, determined to raise awareness about Radvax and its potential. She began writing blog posts and articles detailing her journey, hoping to inspire others facing similar struggles. Her passion for sharing knowledge grew, and she started organizing local meetups for patients interested in learning more about Radvax therapy. Vanessa's voice became a beacon of hope, showcasing the human side of clinical trials and the importance of patient stories in the medical narrative.

Throughout her chronicles, Vanessa emphasized the significance of self-advocacy. She learned to communicate openly with her medical team, asking questions and voicing concerns. This proactive approach not only empowered her but also fostered a sense of partnership with her healthcare providers. As she became more informed about Radvax therapy, Vanessa realized that the journey was as much about education and understanding as it was about treatment. She encouraged others to take ownership of their health, reminding them that knowledge is a potent tool in the battle against chronic illness.

As Vanessa reached the final stages of her Radvax therapy, the results were nothing short of remarkable. Her symptoms had significantly reduced, and she found herself engaging in activities she had long thought impossible. She took up yoga, rediscovered her love for painting, and even started hiking with friends. Each small victory was a testament to her resilience and the effectiveness of the Radvax therapy. Vanessa had transitioned from merely surviving to truly living, and she cherished every moment of her newfound freedom.

In sharing her journey, Vanessa also highlighted the importance of mental health in the healing process. She began attending therapy sessions to address the emotional scars left by years of struggling with her condition. Through these sessions, she learned valuable coping strategies and techniques to manage anxiety and stress. Vanessa found that addressing her mental health was just as crucial as the physical aspect of her treatment, and she advocated for a holistic approach to healing that considered both mind and body.

As Vanessa's Radvax therapy chronicles came to a close, she reflected on the lessons learned throughout her journey. She realized that healing is not a linear process, nor is it solely about the absence of disease. It is about growth, resilience, and the connections forged along the way. Vanessa's story became a testament to the human spirit's capacity to adapt and thrive in the face of adversity. The chronicles of her journey were not just a personal narrative; they became a source of inspiration for countless others navigating their own health challenges. Vanessa understood that her experience could resonate with many who felt isolated in their struggles, and she embraced the role of storyteller with humility and gratitude.

Driven by a newfound purpose, Vanessa established an online platform dedicated to sharing resources about Radvax therapy and autoimmune disorders. She collaborated with healthcare professionals, researchers, and other patients to create a comprehensive hub for information. This platform featured blog posts, video testimonials, and interactive forums where individuals could connect, share advice, and find solace in a community that understood their experiences. Vanessa was committed to ensuring that no one felt alone in their journey, just as she had once felt in her darkest moments.

As her platform grew, Vanessa began to receive messages from individuals around the world who had been touched by her story. Some expressed their gratitude for the insights and encouragement she offered, while others shared their own battles with autoimmune diseases. Each message reinforced her belief in the power of storytelling as a healing tool. Vanessa became a beacon of hope, reminding others that it was possible to confront illness with courage and resilience.

Vanessa also took it upon herself to advocate for further research into Radvax therapy. She reached out to various organizations and participated in panels where she could share her firsthand experience with the treatment. Her voice contributed to a growing conversation about the need for innovative therapies in the realm of autoimmune diseases. Vanessa firmly believed that by raising awareness and sharing data from her own journey, she could help pave the way for future patients to access effective treatments sooner.

In her advocacy work, Vanessa often emphasized the importance of clinical trials in advancing medical science. She encouraged others to consider participation, highlighting how these trials offered hope not just for themselves but for generations to come. By sharing her own experience with the Radvax clinical trial, she illustrated how these studies could lead to breakthroughs that might change lives. Vanessa became an ambassador for the cause, inspiring others to view clinical research as an opportunity rather than a risk.

As Vanessa continued her advocacy, she also prioritized self-care and personal wellness. She learned to navigate the delicate balance between her passion for helping others and tending to her own needs. Meditation, mindfulness, and spending time in nature became integral parts of her routine. She understood that to be an effective advocate, she needed to remain grounded and connected to her own healing journey.

The impact of Vanessa's Radvax therapy chronicles extended beyond her immediate community. She was invited to speak at conferences and health fairs, where she shared her story and the importance of innovative treatments. Her presentations were filled with hope, resilience, and actionable insights that inspired healthcare professionals and patients alike. Vanessa's narrative became a powerful reminder that every individual's journey is unique, yet interconnected within the broader tapestry of human experience.

Through her speaking engagements, Vanessa also highlighted the emotional and psychological aspects of living with chronic illness. She passionately advocated for better mental health support within medical frameworks, emphasizing that emotional well-being is crucial for physical healing. By sharing her own struggles and triumphs, she hoped to destigmatize conversations around mental health and encourage others to seek help when needed.

As the years passed, Vanessa continued to evolve, both as a patient and an advocate. Her Radvax therapy chronicles became a living document of resilience, transformation, and hope. She often reflected on how far she had come, from feeling trapped by her illness to becoming a voice for change and empowerment. Vanessa understood that healing is not just about the absence of symptoms; it is about embracing life in all its complexities and finding joy amidst challenges.

In the end, Vanessa's journey with Radvax therapy was a testament to the power of human connection, knowledge, and advocacy. She had not only transformed her own life but had also sparked a movement that encouraged others to take charge of their health. Vanessa's chronicles would continue to inspire future generations, serving as a reminder that even in the face of adversity, there is always hope, healing, and a chance to reclaim one's life. Her story, woven together with the stories of others, created a rich tapestry of resilience, courage, and the unwavering spirit of humanity.

Chapter Eighteen

A Community Of Warriors

In the heart of a bustling city lies a community that thrives on the strength of its members, a unique collective known as Vanessa's Warriors. This community is composed of family members, friends, and dedicated healthcare professionals who come together to support Vanessa, a young woman facing a significant health challenge. This group embodies resilience, compassion, and hope, creating an environment where love and determination flourish in the face of adversity.

At the center of this community is Vanessa herself, a spirited individual whose courage inspires those around her. Diagnosed with a chronic illness, she has become a beacon of strength for her family and friends. Her journey has brought them closer together, transforming their lives into a shared mission of support and advocacy. Each day presents new challenges, but Vanessa's unwavering positivity reminds everyone of the importance of unity and perseverance.

The family plays a crucial role in Vanessa's Warriors. Each family member has taken on specific responsibilities, creating a well-structured support system. Her parents, for example, are her primary caregivers, balancing their work and personal lives while ensuring that Vanessa receives the best possible care. They attend every doctor's appointment, ask questions, and advocate for her needs, embodying the role of fierce protectors. The siblings also contribute, offering emotional support and companionship, reminding Vanessa that she is never alone in her fight.

The doctors and healthcare professionals involved in Vanessa's care are also integral parts of this community. They are not just medical practitioners; they are partners in her journey. Their expertise, combined with a genuine passion for patient care, fosters an environment of trust and collaboration. Vanessa's doctors take the time to explain treatment options, listen to her concerns, and celebrate her victories, no matter how small. This approach has transformed the clinical experience into a more personal and holistic one.

Support extends beyond the immediate family and medical team. Friends have rallied around Vanessa, creating a broader network of encouragement. They organize events to raise awareness about her condition, participate in fundraising activities to help with medical expenses, and provide emotional support through texts and visits. This solidarity reinforces the notion that community is not just about proximity; it's about shared experiences and unwavering support.

One of the most powerful aspects of Vanessa's Warriors is the sense of purpose that permeates the group. Each member understands the importance of their role in Vanessa's life, and this shared commitment fosters a strong bond among them. They attend workshops and support groups together, gaining insights into coping mechanisms and strategies to navigate the complexities of her illness. This collective learning experience empowers everyone involved, enhancing their ability to support Vanessa effectively.

Coping with a chronic illness can be overwhelming, but Vanessa's community has found ways to infuse joy and positivity into their lives. Regular gatherings, whether they be family dinners or outings with friends, serve as reminders of life's beauty amidst challenges. These moments of laughter and connection provide a necessary reprieve from the stress of medical appointments and treatment regimens, reinforcing the importance of celebrating life's small victories.

In addition to emotional and social support, the community also emphasizes the importance of mental health. Vanessa's Warriors recognize that emotional well-being is just as crucial as physical health. They encourage open conversations about feelings, fears, and hopes, creating a safe space for vulnerability. This dialogue fosters empathy and understanding, allowing each member to express themselves freely without judgment.

As Vanessa continues her journey, her community remains committed to advocating for greater awareness and research into her condition. They participate in campaigns and initiatives aimed at improving the lives of others facing similar challenges. By sharing their experiences and knowledge, they hope to inspire change and contribute to a future where chronic illnesses are better understood and treated.

The resilience of Vanessa's Warriors is a testament to the power of love and support. Their collective efforts remind us that even in the face of adversity, hope can flourish. They embody the idea that no one should face their battles alone, and that together, they can navigate the complexities of health and life. This community, built on trust, compassion, and unwavering support, stands as a powerful example of what it means to be a true warrior.

Ultimately, Vanessa's journey is not just about her fight against illness; it is a story of community, love, and resilience. Each member of her support system plays a vital role in shaping her experience, demonstrating that the bonds of family and friendship can create an indomitable force against life's challenges. Together, they are not just fighting for Vanessa; they are celebrating life, embodying hope, and exemplifying the incredible strength found in unity.

As Vanessa's journey unfolds, the community of Warriors adapts and evolves, constantly finding new ways to support her. They have established a rotating schedule to ensure that someone is always available to accompany Vanessa to her medical appointments, treatments, or even just for a stroll in the park. This system not only alleviates the emotional burden on Vanessa but also strengthens the connections among her family and friends. The act of being present at these appointments allows them to share in her experiences, stay informed about her condition, and lend a listening ear when she needs to express her thoughts and feelings.

In addition to emotional and physical support, the Warriors also emphasize the importance of education. They actively seek out information about Vanessa's condition, attending seminars and reading research articles together. Armed with knowledge, they become better advocates for her care, asking informed questions and challenging assumptions when necessary. This commitment to understanding the intricacies of her illness not only empowers them but also fosters a sense of agency for Vanessa herself. She feels more in control of her health journey, knowing that her community is equipped with the tools to fight alongside her.

The community has also embraced the power of creativity in their support efforts. They have initiated art therapy sessions, allowing Vanessa and her loved ones to express their emotions through painting, drawing, or crafting. These sessions serve as a therapeutic outlet, providing a gentle distraction from the harsh realities of illness. The art created during these sessions often carries deep meaning, reflecting their collective experiences and emotions. These pieces are sometimes displayed at community events or shared on social media, spreading awareness about Vanessa's condition while also inspiring others in similar situations.

Fundraising efforts have become a cornerstone of Vanessa's Warriors. Recognizing the financial strain that chronic illness can impose, the community has organized various events, such as benefit concerts, bake sales, and charity runs. Each event not only raises funds to assist with Vanessa's medical expenses but also serves to strengthen community bonds. Family and friends unite in a common cause, working tirelessly to create successful events that bring people together for both fun and purpose. The support from the broader community illustrates the profound impact Vanessa's story has had, drawing in those who may not even know her personally but are moved by her courage and the dedication of her Warriors.

As the seasons change, so too do the activities of Vanessa's Warriors. They embrace the outdoors, organizing seasonal events like picnics in the park in the summer or cozy gatherings around a fire in the fall. These outings are designed not only to provide a break from the routine of hospital visits and treatments but also to forge lasting memories. Whether it's a simple barbecue or a themed costume party, these moments of joy and laughter serve as powerful reminders of life's fleeting beauty and the importance of cherishing time together. The sense of normalcy amidst the chaos of illness rejuvenates Vanessa and reinforces her belief in the power of love and connection.

Throughout this journey, Vanessa has also become a source of inspiration for her Warriors. Her resilience, humor, and ability to find joy in small moments motivate her family and friends to adopt a similar outlook on life. They often share stories about how Vanessa's spirit has positively impacted their lives, encouraging one another to embrace gratitude and appreciation for everyday experiences. This mutual exchange of encouragement forms an unbreakable bond, reinforcing the idea that they are all in this together, navigating the highs and lows as a united front.

As Vanessa continues to thrive with the support of her community, she has taken on a new role as an advocate for others facing similar challenges. Inspired by her own experiences, she has begun to share her story through social media platforms and local speaking engagements. Her voice resonates with many, shedding light on the realities of living with a chronic illness and the importance of community support. By sharing her journey, Vanessa not only empowers herself but also encourages others to seek out their own Warriors, reminding them that they are not alone in their struggles.

In the end, Vanessa's Warriors exemplify the profound impact of solidarity, love, and resilience. Their journey is a testament to the idea that community is not just a support system; it is a lifeline, a source of strength that can uplift individuals in their darkest moments. Together, they are forging a path of hope, compassion, and unwavering commitment, illustrating that when we stand together, we can conquer even the toughest challenges life throws our way. This community has not only changed the course of Vanessa's life but has also woven a tapestry of connection that will endure long beyond her journey, leaving a legacy of love and support for generations to come.

Chapter Nineteen

Coping With Side Effects

Vanessa sat quietly in her living room, the afternoon sun filtering through the curtains, casting a warm glow that felt almost out of place against the battles she fought within. The diagnosis of kidney cancer had been a deafening blow, reverberating through her life and altering everything she once knew. As she prepared to undergo treatment, she braced herself not just for the physical toll but for the emotional upheaval that came with it. The side effects of chemotherapy loomed large in her mind, like dark clouds threatening to overshadow any flicker of hope.

The first week of treatment was a blur. Vanessa experienced fatigue that felt as if it wrapped around her like a heavy blanket, pulling her down into an abyss of lethargy. Even the simplest tasks, like making a cup of tea or walking to the mailbox, became monumental challenges. She had always prided herself on her independence, but now she found herself leaning on friends and family, feeling both grateful for their support and frustrated by her own limitations. The struggle for normalcy became a daily battle, one that she often lost.

Nausea soon joined the ranks of her unwelcome companions. It was a persistent, gnawing sensation that lingered in the pit of her stomach, casting a shadow over her appetite. Meals that once brought her joy became a source of anxiety. Vanessa tried to muster the strength to eat, convincing herself that nourishment was crucial for her recovery, but each bite felt like swallowing lead. She discovered that ginger tea offered some relief, and she clung to it like a lifeline, hoping to find solace in its warmth.

Sleep, once a refuge, became elusive. The medications swirling in her system played tricks on her mind, and nights were often filled with restless tossing and turning. With her body exhausted yet her mind racing, Vanessa found herself staring at the ceiling, dotting the shadows with thoughts of what lay ahead. She wrestled with the anxiety of the unknown, grappling with fears of the cancer spreading and the thought of her loved ones watching her suffer. It was a heavy burden to bear, one that left her feeling isolated even in a room full of support.

The emotional toll of her diagnosis weighed heavily on her heart. Moments of despair would wash over her like waves, threatening to pull her under. She found herself questioning everything, her past choices, her future, and even her own strength. In those dark moments, Vanessa reached for her journal, pouring out her thoughts and fears onto the pages. Writing became a cathartic release, allowing her to articulate the chaos swirling within and, in turn, providing her a semblance of control over her tumultuous emotions.

As the days turned into weeks, Vanessa began to recognize the importance of self-compassion. She learned to forgive herself for moments of weakness and to accept that it was okay not to be okay. In the mirror, she learned to see beyond the physical changes, the weight loss and the pallor of her skin, and to acknowledge the warrior within. Embracing her vulnerability, she found strength in the shared stories of others who had walked a similar path, drawing inspiration from their journeys.

Amidst the chaos, Vanessa sought solace in her support network. Friends and family rallied around her, organizing meals, sending flowers, and offering a listening ear. Their love became a balm for her soul, reminding her of the connections that mattered most. She learned to lean on them, to share her fears and frustrations, and to allow their kindness to uplift her spirit. Each gesture, no matter how small, became a reminder that she was not alone in her fight.

In the quiet moments, she turned to mindfulness and meditation, discovering a way to center herself amidst the storm. Breathing exercises became a ritual, helping her reclaim a sense of calm when anxiety threatened to spiral out of control. She learned to focus on the present, to relish the beauty of small moments, a warm cup of tea, the sound of laughter, the gentle rustle of leaves outside her window. These fragments of joy became her anchor, grounding her in the reality that life still held beauty, even in its darkest chapters.

As Vanessa continued her treatment, she realized that healing was not a linear journey. There were good days and bad days, moments of triumph and moments of despair. She learned to celebrate the small victories, whether it was a day free from nausea or a brief respite from fatigue. Each step forward, no matter how insignificant it seemed, became a testament to her resilience. The fight against cancer was not just about the physical battle; it was also about nurturing her spirit and embracing hope.

In the face of uncertainty, Vanessa discovered the profound importance of hope. It became her guiding light, a flicker that refused to be extinguished, even in the darkest of times. She surrounded herself with positive affirmations, reminding herself that she was more than her diagnosis. Hope became her shield against despair, empowering her to envision a future beyond cancer.

As Vanessa navigated the complexities of her diagnosis, she found herself drawn to the stories of others who had faced similar battles. Online forums and support groups became her refuge, where she connected with individuals who shared their experiences and offered encouragement. Their resilience inspired her, and with each story she read, Vanessa felt a sense of camaraderie wash over her. It was a realization that she was part of a larger community. A collective of warriors who understood the weight of her journey and had emerged stronger on the other side.

One evening, while scrolling through a support group, Vanessa came across a post that caught her attention. A woman shared her triumph over cancer, detailing the small rituals she had adopted to reclaim joy amidst the struggle. Intrigued, Vanessa decided to implement some of these practices in her own life. She began to create a daily gratitude list, jotting down three things each day that made her smile, no matter how minute. This simple exercise shifted her perspective, allowing her to focus on the positive aspects of her life, even on days when the shadows loomed large.

As weeks turned into months, Vanessa found herself stepping out of her comfort zone. She signed up for gentle yoga classes designed for cancer patients, hoping to find some relief from her physical ailments. The first class was daunting, filled with unfamiliar poses and hesitant participants, but as she settled onto her mat, she felt an unexpected sense of peace. The instructor's soothing voice guided them through each movement, encouraging them to listen to their bodies. With every breath, Vanessa felt a release, a letting go of tension and fear that had gripped her for so long.

The camaraderie in the yoga class quickly became a source of strength. Vanessa forged friendships with others who were navigating their own health journeys. They shared laughter and tears, offering support and understanding that transcended the confines of their illness. These connections became a vital lifeline, reminding her that even in the depths of hardship, she was surrounded by love and understanding. The sense of belonging fostered a newfound courage within her. A realization that she could lean on others without feeling like a burden.

As her treatment progressed, Vanessa also became more attuned to her body's needs. She experimented with nutrition, seeking out foods that could bolster her immune system and provide energy. Cooking became an act of self-care, and she found joy in preparing colorful, wholesome meals. Each dish she created was infused with intention, a reminder that she was nourishing not just her body but her spirit. Sharing meals with friends and family became a cherished ritual, as they gathered around the table to celebrate the small victories of life amidst the uncertainty.

However, not every day was filled with light and laughter. There were still moments when the weight of fear threatened to overtake her. Vanessa experienced waves of sadness that crashed over her unexpectedly, reminding her of the fragility of life. During these times, she turned to her journal once more, pouring out her heart onto the pages. Writing became a powerful outlet, allowing her to confront her fears head-on, and in doing so, she often found clarity.

Through the darkness, she discovered that vulnerability was not a sign of weakness but a testament to her strength and authenticity.

One afternoon, as she sat in her backyard, soaking in the sun's warmth, Vanessa felt a shift within her. The once overwhelming fear of her cancer diagnosis began to transform into a fierce determination. She realized that while she could not control the outcome, she could control her response. This newfound mindset propelled her to advocate for herself, asking questions during appointments and seeking second opinions. Empowered by knowledge, she felt more like a participant in her journey rather than a passive observer, an active player in the game of life.

With each passing day, Vanessa's journey became a tapestry woven with threads of resilience, hope, and connection. She learned to embrace the uncertainty that lay ahead, recognizing that life's unpredictability was not something to fear but to cherish. The moments of joy became more vivid, and she found herself savoring the laughter of friends, the warmth of family, and the simple beauty of nature. The side effects of her treatment were still present, but they no longer defined her existence; she was more than her illness.

As Vanessa continued to share her journey on social media, she became an unexpected source of hope for others. Friends and acquaintances reached out, expressing gratitude for her honesty and vulnerability. Her willingness to share the raw, unfiltered aspects of her experience resonated with many, reminding them that they were not alone in their struggles. It was a profound realization that her battle could serve as a beacon of light for others, and in turn, it fueled her own spirit, igniting a sense of purpose.

Eventually, the day came when Vanessa received the news she had been hoping for: the cancer was in remission. Tears streamed down her face as she absorbed the weight of the words, a mix of disbelief and gratitude flooding her heart.

Chapter Twenty

When Hope Feels Distant

Vanessa had always been a vibrant person, filled with dreams and aspirations. She is a dedicated mother, a passionate grandmother, and an avid hard worker. Her life was full of joy and laughter, but everything changed when she experienced a persistent pain in her side. After a series of doctor visits and tests, she received the devastating diagnosis of kidney cancer. The words echoed in her mind, leaving her feeling both numb and terrified. Hope felt distant, overshadowed by the uncertainty that loomed over her future.

The initial shock was overwhelming. Vanessa found herself grappling with a whirlwind of emotions, fear, anger, and an overwhelming sense of isolation. She had heard stories of cancer fighters, but now she was one of them. The thought of undergoing surgery, Radvax Therapy, and the possibility of not being there for her surviving children weighed heavily on her heart. She felt as if she were trapped in a dark tunnel, with no light to guide her. Friends and family rallied around her, but their well-meaning words often felt hollow in the face of her reality.

In the weeks that followed her diagnosis, Vanessa took a deep breath and resolved to educate herself about her condition. She spent hours reading about kidney cancer, treatment options, and stories of survival. Knowledge became her lifeline, a way to regain a semblance of control in an otherwise chaotic situation. She discovered support groups both online and in her community, where she found solace in connecting with others who shared her struggles. Each story she heard reminded her that she was not alone, and that there was a glimmer of hope in the darkest of times.

As Vanessa prepared for her surgery, she found a renewed sense of purpose. She began to journal her thoughts and feelings, pouring her heart onto the pages. Writing became her therapy, a way to confront her fears and articulate her hopes. She penned letters to her children, expressing her love and the lessons she wanted to impart, should she not be there to tell them in person. This act of vulnerability strengthened her resolve and served as a reminder of what she was fighting for. In her darkest moments, her children became a beacon of hope, motivating her to keep going.

Surgery day arrived, and Vanessa was a bundle of nerves. As she lay on the operating table, she focused on her breathing, allowing herself to visualize a positive outcome. The support of her family and friends bolstered her spirits, and she clung to the belief that this was a necessary step toward healing. When she awoke, groggy but alive, she felt a surge of gratitude. The first hurdle had been crossed, but the road ahead was still fraught with challenges.

Recovery was not easy. The physical pain was accompanied by emotional turmoil as she navigated the aftermath of her surgery. There were days when the weight of despair felt unbearable, and hope seemed like a distant memory. Yet, Vanessa found strength in her support network. Friends organized meal trains and offered to take care of her children, allowing her to focus on her healing. Slowly, she learned to accept help and lean on those who loved her. It was a lesson in vulnerability that she had never anticipated but came to cherish.

As she began her Radvax Therapy treatment, Vanessa faced the harsh reality of side effects, fatigue, nausea, and hair loss. Each session felt like a battle, but she was determined to fight. She sought out alternative therapies, like meditation and yoga, to help manage her stress and regain some sense of normalcy. With each treatment, she reminded herself that she was not defined by her illness. She was a warrior, fighting for her life and her family. The mantra "This too shall pass" became her guiding light.

Throughout her journey, Vanessa found inspiration in the stories of fellow cancer survivors. She attended support group meetings, where she connected with others who had faced similar battles. Their resilience ignited a fire within her, reminding her that hope was not a fleeting concept but a powerful force that could fuel her recovery. She began to share her own story, finding strength in vulnerability and inspiring others along the way. Each connection reaffirmed her belief that even in the face of adversity, hope could thrive.

As the months passed, Vanessa's perspective on life shifted. The once-distant hope began to feel tangible as she celebrated small victories, her children's laughter, the ability to take a short walk, or simply enjoying a sunny day. Each moment became a reminder of the beauty that could still exist despite her circumstances. She learned to embrace gratitude, finding joy in the little things that often went unnoticed. Her journey became a testament to the resilience of the human spirit, and she vowed to live fully, no matter the outcome.

Eventually, Vanessa received the news she had been praying for. Her cancer was in remission. The relief washed over her like a warm wave, but it was accompanied by a newfound understanding of life's fragility. The experience had changed her in profound ways, and she knew that she would never take another moment for granted. The journey through kidney cancer had taught her the depth of her strength and the importance of community. As she reflected on her path, she realized that while the physical battle was over, the emotional and psychological journey was just beginning. She had emerged not only as a survivor but as an advocate for others facing similar struggles.

With her newfound lease on life, Vanessa felt a deep calling to share her story more widely. She began volunteering with local cancer support organizations, providing mentorship and encouragement to newly diagnosed patients. She understood the fear and uncertainty that enveloped them, and she wanted to be a beacon of hope, just as others had been for her. Through her outreach, she found purpose in helping others navigate their journeys. In doing so, she not only honored her own experience but also contributed to a community that had become so integral to her healing.

Vanessa also started engaging in sharing her story at events and cancer awareness seminars. Each time she listened, she felt a sense of empowerment wash over her. Their voices resonated with her and everyone in the audience, and she could see the impact of the words reflected in their faces. It became clear to her that sharing her journey was not just about her own healing; it was about inspiring others to hold onto hope, even when it seemed elusive. Through her vulnerability, she was forging connections and fostering a sense of solidarity among those battling cancer.

As the seasons changed, so did Vanessa. She began to embrace a healthier lifestyle, altering her diet and incorporating exercise into her daily routine. Running, which had once been a source of joy, gradually became a symbol of resilience. She would lace up her sneakers and hit the trails, feeling the rhythm of her heartbeat as a reminder of her strength. Each mile she completed felt like a victory, a manifestation of her survival and determination to thrive. Running transformed from a mere hobby into a celebration of life, a way for her to reclaim her body and spirit.

The journey of recovery was not without its setbacks. There were days when anxiety crept in, and she found herself revisiting the dark moments of her diagnosis. However, Vanessa learned to recognize these feelings as part of the healing process. She practiced mindfulness and gratitude, reflecting on the progress she had made. With each passing day, she grew more adept at managing her emotions, understanding that hope does not always mean the absence of fear. Instead, it was about finding strength in the face of uncertainty and allowing herself to feel joy alongside her apprehension.

As Vanessa stood at the finish line of a local charity run dedicated to cancer research, she was overwhelmed with emotion. Surrounded by friends, family, and fellow survivors, she felt a profound sense of belonging. This was more than just a race; it was a celebration of life, hope, and resilience. In that moment, Vanessa recognized that hope was no longer a distant concept, but a vibrant part of her existence. She had transformed her journey through kidney cancer into a story of empowerment, reminding herself and others that even in the darkest of times, hope can illuminate the path forward.

Chapter Twenty One

The Importance of Self-Care

Vanessa's journey with kidney cancer is a profound testament to the importance of self-care during challenging times. Cancer can be an overwhelming experience, not just physically but emotionally and mentally as well. For Vanessa, self-care has become an essential part of her routine, helping her navigate the complexities of her diagnosis and treatment while maintaining her sense of self and well-being.

First and foremost, self-care allows Vanessa to take control of her health during a time when she may feel powerless. By prioritizing her own needs, she can manage her symptoms more effectively and engage in her treatment plan with a positive mindset. This proactive approach can lead to better health outcomes, as patients who actively participate in their care often report higher satisfaction and improved quality of life.

Physical self-care is particularly crucial for Vanessa as she undergoes treatment. Maintaining a balanced diet, staying hydrated, and getting regular exercise can help bolster her immune system and keep her energy levels up. Simple activities, like gentle walks or yoga, not only help Vanessa stay physically fit but also promote mental clarity and emotional stability, enabling her to cope better with the stresses of her condition.

Mental and emotional self-care are equally important for Vanessa. Cancer can evoke a wide range of emotions, from fear and anxiety to anger and sadness. By engaging in activities that bring her joy and relaxation, such as reading, meditation, or pursuing hobbies, Vanessa can create a sanctuary for her mind. This mental respite is crucial for maintaining a positive outlook, which has been shown to influence overall health and recovery.

Social support plays a vital role in Vanessa's self-care strategy. Connecting with friends, family, or support groups provides her with an outlet for sharing her feelings and experiences. These interactions can serve as a reminder that she is not alone in her fight against cancer. Building a strong support network can also help combat feelings of isolation and loneliness, which are common among cancer patients.

Additionally, self-care practices can help Vanessa cope with the side effects of treatment. Many cancer therapies come with a host of physical repercussions, including fatigue, nausea, and pain. By engaging in self-care routines, such as warm baths, relaxation techniques, or gentle stretching, she can alleviate some of these symptoms. This attention to her body and its needs can make her treatment journey more manageable and less daunting.

Spiritual self-care is another aspect that Vanessa finds invaluable. Whether through prayer, meditation, or spending time in nature, connecting with her spiritual side can provide Vanessa with comfort and strength. This grounding practice can help her find meaning in her experience and foster resilience, enabling her to face the challenges of cancer with grace and determination.

Moreover, self-care empowers Vanessa to set boundaries. She learns to listen to her body and recognize when she needs to rest or when to say no to social obligations that may feel overwhelming. This newfound assertiveness not only helps her manage her energy but also reinforces her sense of autonomy in a situation where she might otherwise feel vulnerable.

It is also essential for Vanessa to educate herself about kidney cancer and available treatment options. Knowledge is a powerful tool that can help demystify the disease and reduce fear. By staying informed, Vanessa can make empowered decisions regarding her treatment and advocate for herself effectively, aligning her care with her personal values and preferences.

In the broader context, Vanessa's commitment to self-care can serve as an inspiration for others facing similar battles. By sharing her experiences and strategies, she can encourage fellow cancer patients to prioritize their well-being. This ripple effect can foster a sense of community and support among those navigating the challenges of cancer, highlighting the collective strength that emerges when individuals prioritize self-care.

Finally, Vanessa's journey underscores the importance of self-compassion. Cancer is a tough battle, and it's easy to succumb to feelings of guilt or inadequacy. By treating herself with kindness and understanding, Vanessa can cultivate resilience and foster a more balanced perspective on her experience. Ultimately, her commitment to self-care not only aids in her recovery but also enriches her life, allowing her to find joy and purpose even in the face of adversity.

In addition to the physical, mental, and emotional benefits, self-care provides Vanessa with a sense of normalcy amidst the chaos of her cancer diagnosis. Daily routines and activities that she loves can serve as anchors, helping her feel grounded. Whether it's enjoying her morning coffee, tending to her garden, or engaging in creative projects, these moments contribute to her overall sense of identity and continuity. They remind her that life exists beyond the diagnosis, allowing her to cultivate joy in small, meaningful ways.

Self-care also encourages Vanessa to practice mindfulness, a technique that has gained recognition for its positive effects on mental health. By being present in each moment, she can reduce anxiety about future uncertainties related to her health. Mindfulness practices, such as deep breathing or guided meditation, can help Vanessa manage stress and foster a sense of peace. This awareness allows her to observe her thoughts and emotions without judgment, providing a safe space to process her experiences.

As Vanessa delves deeper into her self-care practices, she discovers the power of journaling. Writing down her thoughts, fears, and hopes serves as a therapeutic outlet, enabling her to articulate feelings that may be difficult to express aloud. Journaling also allows her to track her progress, celebrate small victories, and reflect on her journey. This practice can be a vital tool for emotional healing, helping her to navigate the ups and downs of treatment with greater clarity and resilience.

In recognizing the importance of self-care, Vanessa also learns to seek professional support when needed. Engaging with a therapist or counselor can provide her with additional coping strategies tailored to her unique situation. Mental health professionals can help her process the emotional toll of cancer, teaching her techniques to manage anxiety and depression. Seeking help is a sign of strength, and Vanessa's willingness to do so highlights her commitment to her well-being.

Moreover, the role of nutrition in Vanessa's self-care cannot be overstated. She learns to appreciate the healing properties of food, opting for a diet rich in fruits, vegetables, whole grains, and lean proteins. Proper nutrition not only supports her physical health but also contributes to her emotional well-being. As she experiments with new recipes and cooking techniques, Vanessa finds joy in nourishing herself, creating a positive relationship with food that empowers her on her healing journey.

Connections with others facing similar challenges can also enhance Vanessa's self-care routine. By participating in support groups, whether in-person or online, she can share her experiences, gain insights, and receive encouragement from those who truly understand her situation. These connections foster a sense of belonging and validation, reminding her that she is part of a larger community of survivors and fighters. The shared wisdom and camaraderie can offer comfort and motivation as she navigates her path.

Vanessa's self-care journey also involves embracing creativity as a form of expression and healing. Engaging in artistic pursuits, whether it's painting, crafting, or writing poetry, allows her to channel her emotions into something tangible. This creative outlet can serve as a cathartic experience, providing her with a sense of accomplishment and fulfillment. By allowing her artistic side to flourish, Vanessa can transcend her circumstances and find beauty even in the midst of struggle.

As Vanessa continues to prioritize self-care, she becomes more attuned to her body's signals. Listening to her physical needs helps her to recognize when to rest, when to seek medical attention, and when to celebrate her strengths. This heightened awareness fosters a deeper connection with herself, allowing her to respond to her body with compassion rather than frustration. It encourages a holistic approach to her health, recognizing that mind, body, and spirit are intricately intertwined.

Ultimately, Vanessa's commitment to self-care serves as a beacon of hope not only for herself but for others impacted by kidney cancer. Her journey illustrates that self-care is not a luxury but a necessity, especially during times of adversity. By embracing self-care, Vanessa empowers herself to navigate the complexities of cancer with grace and resilience, inspiring those around her to prioritize their own well-being. Her story is a reminder that, even in the face of life's most significant challenges, it is possible to cultivate joy, connection, and strength through the practice of self-care.

Creating a new normal is a profound journey for Vanessa as she learns to navigate life after her kidney cancer diagnosis. This transition involves redefining her daily routines, relationships, and sense of self, all while coping with the realities of her illness. It is a process marked by both challenges and opportunities for growth, enabling Vanessa to discover resilience and strength she never knew she possessed.

Initially, Vanessa grapples with the disorientation that often accompanies a cancer diagnosis. The life she once knew has been upended, filled with medical appointments, treatment schedules, and the uncertainties of illness. In this tumultuous period, she realizes the importance of establishing new routines that cater to her evolving needs. By prioritizing consistency in her daily life, such as regular meal times, exercise, and relaxation practices, Vanessa begins to create a sense of stability amidst the chaos.

One of the key aspects of Vanessa's new normal is her commitment to self-care. She recognizes that caring for her physical, emotional, and mental well-being is not just beneficial but essential for her recovery. By integrating practices such as meditation, journaling, and gentle movement into her daily routine, she cultivates a nurturing environment for herself. This newfound focus on self-care not only helps her cope with the side effects of treatment but also fosters a deeper connection to her own body.

Social connections play a vital role in Vanessa's journey toward creating a new normal. She learns to lean on her friends and family for support, openly sharing her experiences and feelings. By fostering open communication, she allows her loved ones to understand her needs better, leading to stronger bonds and a more profound sense of community. In turn, these relationships provide her with emotional comfort, reminding her that she is not alone in her fight against cancer.

In addition to nurturing existing relationships, Vanessa embraces the idea of building new connections. She seeks out support groups and communities of fellow cancer survivors, discovering a wealth of shared experiences and wisdom. These interactions serve as a powerful reminder that while her journey is uniquely hers, others have walked similar paths. The camaraderie she finds in these spaces fosters a sense of belonging, reinforcing her resilience and determination.

As Vanessa continues on her journey, she begins to redefine her sense of identity. The label of "cancer patient" can be overwhelming, but she actively works to reclaim her narrative. By engaging in creative outlets, such as painting, writing, or photography, she expresses her emotions and reaffirms her individuality. These artistic pursuits allow her to explore her identity beyond cancer, helping her to embrace a more holistic view of herself.

Vanessa also recognizes the importance of setting boundaries as she creates her new normal. She learns to say no to obligations that drain her energy or add unnecessary stress to her life. By prioritizing her well-being, she cultivates a lifestyle that aligns with her values and needs. This newfound assertiveness empowers her to take control of her life, reinforcing the idea that it is okay to prioritize herself during this challenging time.

A pivotal part of Vanessa's journey involves finding purpose in her experiences. As she reflects on her journey, she discovers a passion for advocacy and education about kidney cancer. By sharing her story and insights with others, she inspires hope and raises awareness. This sense of purpose becomes a driving force in her life, allowing her to transform her struggles into a source of strength for herself and others.

In the midst of creating her new normal, Vanessa also learns to embrace uncertainty. Living with cancer often means facing the unknown, but she becomes more comfortable with this reality over time. Through mindfulness practices and acceptance, she develops a deeper understanding of impermanence. This shift in perspective empowers her to focus on the present moment, finding joy and gratitude in the everyday experiences that make life rich.

As her new normal continues to take shape, Vanessa celebrates her small victories. Whether it's completing a challenging workout, finishing a creative project, or simply enjoying a day without overwhelming anxiety, she acknowledges her progress. These moments of celebration serve as reminders of her strength and resilience, reinforcing her belief that she can not only cope with her diagnosis but thrive in spite of it.

Ultimately, Vanessa's journey of creating a new normal is a testament to the human spirit's capacity for adaptation and growth. Through self-care, connection, creativity, and purpose, she cultivates a life that reflects her values and aspirations, even in the face of adversity. Vanessa's experience serves as an inspiration for others navigating similar challenges, illustrating that it is possible to forge a new path and find meaning in life after cancer. Her story is a powerful reminder that, while the journey may be fraught with difficulties, it can also be rich with beauty, connection, and hope.

Chapter Twenty Two

Creating a New Normal

Vanessa had always viewed her life as a colorful tapestry woven with dreams, ambitions, and cherished moments. As a devoted mother, she thrived on creativity and connection. But when she was diagnosed with kidney cancer, that vivid tapestry felt ripped apart, leaving her grappling with fear and uncertainty. The diagnosis was a seismic shock, shattering her sense of normalcy. However, Vanessa's spirit was resilient, and rather than allowing the diagnosis to define her, she chose to create a new normal. One that embraced both her struggles and her strengths.

The first step in Vanessa's journey was acknowledging her emotions. Initially, she felt overwhelmed by fear and sadness, but she recognized that these feelings were valid. She began journaling her thoughts and emotions, using the pages as a safe space to express her fears, hopes, and dreams. Writing became a therapeutic outlet, helping her process her feelings about her diagnosis and the uncertain road ahead. Each entry was a step toward reclaiming her narrative, allowing her to confront her reality without being consumed by it.

Next, Vanessa focused on education. She immersed herself in understanding kidney cancer, researching treatment options and speaking with healthcare professionals. Knowledge became her armor, empowering her to make informed decisions about her treatment plan. Armed with information, she felt more in control, transforming her fear into proactive engagement. She learned about nutrition, exercise, and the importance of mental well-being during treatment, which became essential components of her new normal.

As she began treatment, Vanessa found solace in a support group of fellow cancer patients. These meetings became a lifeline, providing her with a sense of belonging and understanding. Sharing her journey with others who understood the weight of her experience helped her feel less isolated. Together, they celebrated small victories, shared laughs, and provided comfort during difficult times. This newfound community reinforced the idea that vulnerability could be a source of strength, not weakness.

In the midst of her treatments, Vanessa rediscovered her passion for life. She transformed her tiny home into a sanctuary, a place where she could escape the harsh realities of her diagnosis. Her life became her refuge, allowing her to express emotions that words often failed to capture. She began an article titled "Resilience," channeling her journey into vibrant colors of newfound strength, hope and peace. Each word was a testament to her fight, a reminder that beauty could emerge from pain. The article not only helped her heal but also became a source of inspiration for others facing similar battles.

Vanessa also embraced a healthier lifestyle, viewing her diagnosis as an opportunity for transformation. She consulted with nutritionists and began incorporating wholesome foods into her diet, focusing on nourishing her body and boosting her immune system. Regular exercise became part of her routine; she found joy in yoga and nature walks, activities that not only strengthened her body but also calmed her mind. This newfound commitment to self-care became a cornerstone of her new normal, promoting both physical and emotional healing.

Mindfulness emerged as another essential element in Vanessa's journey. She began practicing meditation, learning to find peace in the present moment. Each session allowed her to quiet the noise of anxiety and fear, grounding her as she navigated the uncertainties of her illness. Through mindfulness, Vanessa discovered the power of gratitude, focusing on the small joys in her daily life. A warm cup of tea, the laughter of her children, the beauty of a sunset. These moments became anchors, reminding her of the life she was fighting for.

As she progressed through treatment, Vanessa felt a shift within herself. The fear that once loomed large began to diminish, replaced by a growing sense of hope and determination. She started to advocate for herself, asking questions and voicing concerns during medical appointments. This newfound assertiveness not only empowered her but also inspired others in her support group. Vanessa realized that reclaiming her life meant taking an active role in her health journey, refusing to be a passive participant in her own story.

In her quest to create a new normal, Vanessa also focused on strengthening her relationships. She communicated openly with her family about her needs, fears, and aspirations. This transparency fostered deeper connections, allowing her loved ones to support her in meaningful ways. Family gatherings turned into cherished moments filled with laughter and love, creating a safe haven where she could be vulnerable without judgment. Vanessa learned that vulnerability could deepen intimacy, and this realization became a source of comfort and strength.

As the months passed, Vanessa's journey through cancer became a profound exploration of resilience. She emerged from her treatments not just as a survivor but as a transformed individual who had learned to embrace life in all its complexities. The experience taught her to savor each moment, to find joy in the little things, and to approach challenges with a renewed sense of purpose. Her art flourished, infused with a deeper understanding of the fragility and beauty of life.

Ultimately, Vanessa's journey was not just about overcoming cancer; it was about creating a new normal that honored her past while embracing her present and future. Through her experiences, she cultivated a profound appreciation for life, recognizing that every day was a gift. Even the simplest moments became meaningful as she learned to celebrate small victories, whether it was completing a painting, enjoying a family meal, or simply taking a walk in the park. Vanessa's perspective shifted; she no longer took life for granted. Instead, she approached each day with intention and gratitude, knowing that the journey was just as important as the destination.

In sharing her journey, Vanessa felt a calling to give back to others facing similar battles. Inspired by the support she received, she decided to organize art workshops for cancer patients and survivors. These workshops became a space for healing and self-expression, where participants could explore their emotions through creativity. Vanessa created a safe environment where individuals felt empowered to share their stories through art. The experience not only helped others heal but also deepened her own understanding of resilience and community.

As she continued to navigate her new normal, Vanessa became increasingly involved in advocacy work for cancer awareness and research. She collaborated with local organizations to raise funds and awareness about kidney cancer, sharing her story to educate others about the importance of early detection and treatment options. Through public speaking engagements and community events, she inspired countless individuals to take an active role in their health. Vanessa became a beacon of hope, demonstrating that it was possible to find purpose even in the face of adversity.

Vanessa's journey also inspired her to reconnect with her artistic roots on a deeper level. She began to explore new mediums and styles, pushing the boundaries of her creativity. Her art reflected not only her personal struggles but also her triumphs, embodying the spirit of resilience that defined her. She held exhibitions showcasing her work, where each piece told a story of hope, courage, and transformation. The feedback from viewers was overwhelmingly positive, with many expressing how her art resonated with their own experiences.

As time went on, Vanessa learned to balance her life as a survivor and her role as a mother. She became more present with her children, teaching them the value of gratitude and resilience. They often painted together, using art as a way to bond and express their emotions. Vanessa shared her journey openly with her kids, ensuring they understood the importance of health, empathy, and living life to the fullest. This connection not only strengthened their relationship but also instilled in them a sense of purpose and compassion.

The experience of living with cancer also deepened Vanessa's appreciation for her friendships. She learned to lean on her friends for support and to be vulnerable in her relationships. This openness allowed her to forge deeper connections, and her friends rallied around her, providing emotional and practical support throughout her treatments. In return, Vanessa became a more supportive friend, offering her time and energy to others in need. She learned that the act of giving was just as important as receiving, creating a cycle of love and support.

As she reflected on her journey, Vanessa realized that the cancer diagnosis, while profoundly challenging, had sparked a transformation that she never could have anticipated. It had pushed her to confront her fears, embrace vulnerability, and cultivate resilience. Through her art, advocacy, and community involvement, she had not only reclaimed her life but had also become a catalyst for change in the lives of others. Vanessa had crafted a new normal—one that was rich with purpose, creativity, and connection.

Emerging from this experience, Vanessa felt a renewed sense of purpose. She understood that life was not just about surviving but about thriving. Her journey had taught her that even in the face of adversity, it was possible to create beauty and meaning. With every brushstroke, every workshop, and every story shared, she celebrated her survival and the lives of those still fighting. Vanessa was not just a survivor of kidney cancer; she was a warrior, an artist, and a beacon of hope, inspiring others to find their light amidst the darkness.

Chapter Twenty Three

Transformative Moments

Vanessa's journey with kidney cancer began unexpectedly during a routine check-up. She was a vibrant, active individual who had always prioritized her health. However, a series of troubling symptoms—persistent fatigue, unexplained weight loss, and occasional flank pain—prompted her doctor to recommend further investigation. The diagnosis came as a shock: renal cell carcinoma. In that moment, Vanessa's world shifted. The vibrant colors of her life dulled as she grappled with the harsh reality of a cancer diagnosis, forcing her to confront her mortality and reevaluate her priorities.

The initial phase of Vanessa's transformation was marked by disbelief and fear. She spent countless sleepless nights contemplating the implications of her diagnosis. Would she be able to continue her career? How would her family cope? The uncertainty loomed over her like a dark cloud. However, this period of introspection also ignited a fierce determination within her. Instead of succumbing to despair, Vanessa resolved to take control of her situation. She immersed herself in research, educating herself about kidney cancer, treatment options, and lifestyle changes that could bolster her health.

As Vanessa began her treatment journey, she encountered a myriad of emotions. The side effects of chemotherapy were daunting, but she found solace in the support of her loved ones. Her family rallied around her, providing a strong network of encouragement and love. This collective strength became a transformative moment for Vanessa. She realized that vulnerability was not a weakness; rather, it was an invitation for deeper connections. The experience allowed her to lean on others and embrace the beauty of human compassion.

With each session of chemotherapy, Vanessa discovered an inner resilience she never knew existed. The physical toll of the treatment was immense, but it was during these challenging days that she began to appreciate the small victories. A good day, where she felt energetic enough to take a short walk or enjoy a meal with her family, became a source of immense joy. This shift in perspective allowed her to cultivate gratitude in daily life, transforming mundane moments into cherished memories. The power of gratitude became a guiding principle in her journey toward healing.

As Vanessa navigated her treatment, she also sought out alternative therapies that complemented her medical regimen. Mindfulness practices, yoga, and meditation became vital components of her daily routine. These practices not only helped her manage stress but also fostered a deeper connection to her body and spirit. Through mindfulness, she learned to listen to her body's signals, honoring its needs instead of pushing through pain. This newfound awareness transformed her approach to health and wellness, leading to a more balanced lifestyle.

One of Vanessa's most profound transformative moments came when she participated in a cancer support group. Initially hesitant, she soon discovered the healing power of shared experiences. Listening to others share their stories of resilience and hope inspired her to open up about her own struggles. The group became a safe space where vulnerability thrived, and where she learned to articulate her fears and aspirations. This communal healing experience reinforced her belief in the importance of connection and the strength that comes from shared adversity.

As Vanessa's treatment progressed, the landscape of her life began to shift once more. With the cancer in remission, she felt a renewed sense of purpose. The struggle had forged a new identity within her—one that was more authentic and grounded. She became an advocate for cancer awareness and education, sharing her story to inspire others facing similar battles. This shift from patient to advocate marked a significant transformation in her life, illustrating how adversity could lead to empowerment and purpose.

Vanessa also began to reassess her relationships. Some connections deepened, while others faded. She learned to prioritize those who uplifted her and distanced herself from negativity. This selective approach to relationships was liberating. It allowed her to focus on genuine connections that nourished her soul. Through this process, Vanessa discovered the importance of surrounding herself with positivity, a lesson that would continue to serve her well beyond her cancer journey.

The experience of battling kidney cancer also transformed Vanessa's perspective on time. She became acutely aware of the fleeting nature of life and the importance of living in the present. This realization encouraged her to embark on new adventures, whether it was traveling to places she had always dreamed of visiting or simply enjoying spontaneous outings with friends. Each day became an opportunity to create lasting memories, reinforcing her belief that life is meant to be celebrated.

As Vanessa continued her journey of healing, she embraced a holistic approach to her well-being. Nutrition, exercise, and mental health became integral parts of her life. She learned to cook nutritious meals that fueled her body and mind, discovering joy in preparing food for herself and her family. This transformation extended beyond just physical health; it also fostered a deeper understanding of self-care and the importance of nurturing her entire being.

Ultimately, Vanessa's journey with kidney cancer was not merely a story of struggle; it was a narrative of profound transformation. She emerged from her experience not only as a survivor but as a beacon of hope for others.

story became an embodiment of resilience, illustrating how one can find strength in vulnerability and purpose in adversity. Vanessa learned that life is not just about enduring challenges but also about embracing the lessons they bring. She became a living testament to the idea that transformation often arises from hardship, and that facing one's fears can lead to growth beyond imagination.

Empowered by her experience, Vanessa sought to share her newfound wisdom with a broader audience. She began writing a blog chronicling her journey through cancer, capturing the raw emotions, struggles, and triumphs along the way. Her words resonated with many, providing comfort and inspiration to those navigating similar paths. Through her writing, she fostered a sense of community among readers, creating a space where shared experiences could flourish and support could be found. This act of vulnerability not only helped others but also deepened her own healing process, reinforcing the idea that connection is a powerful tool in overcoming adversity.

Vanessa's advocacy efforts extended beyond her blog. She volunteered with local cancer organizations, participating in awareness campaigns and fundraising events. Engaging with fellow survivors and their families became a vital aspect of her life. Through these interactions, she found a sense of belonging and purpose, as if her journey was part of something much larger. This work reminded her that while her battle was personal, it was also a collective fight against cancer. One that required community, support, and shared determination.

In her personal life, Vanessa's relationships flourished in unexpected ways. The people she had once taken for granted became sources of deep connection and understanding. Family gatherings transformed into celebrations of life, where laughter and love filled the spaces once occupied by fear and uncertainty. Vanessa's journey taught her the importance of cherishing these moments, leading her to prioritize quality time with loved ones. She organized get-togethers that celebrated not only her survival but also the relationships that sustained her throughout her battle.

As Vanessa continued to thrive, she also realized the importance of self-compassion. The road to recovery was not linear; there were days when she felt overwhelmed by anxiety or sadness. Instead of pushing these feelings away, she learned to embrace them, understanding that healing is a multifaceted process. This acceptance allowed her to cultivate a more profound sense of peace, recognizing that it was okay to feel vulnerable sometimes. By practicing self-compassion, she created a safe space for herself to navigate the complexities of her emotions, ultimately leading to a more balanced and resilient mindset.

Through her experience, Vanessa also discovered the power of gratitude in a deeper sense. It became a daily practice for her to reflect on the things she was thankful for, no matter how small. This practice transformed her outlook on life, allowing her to appreciate the beauty in the ordinary. She found joy in a morning cup of coffee, the warmth of the sun on her skin, and the laughter of children playing in her neighborhood. Gratitude became a lens through which she viewed the world, enabling her to cultivate happiness and contentment even amidst life's challenges.

As Vanessa looked back on her transformative journey, she recognized that her experience with kidney cancer was not merely a chapter in her life; it was a catalyst for profound change. She had emerged from the darkness with a renewed sense of purpose, a deeper understanding of her own strength, and an unwavering commitment to living life to its fullest. Vanessa's story became a beacon of hope for others, illustrating that even in the face of the most daunting challenges, transformation is possible. It is a journey marked by resilience, connection, and an enduring spirit—one that continues to inspire not only herself but all those who hear her story.

Chapter Twenty Four

Celebrating Small Victories

Vanessa had always been a vibrant soul, someone who relished in the small joys of life. However, her world was turned upside down when she was diagnosed with stage 4 kidney cancer. At first, the news was overwhelming, and the weight of uncertainty pressed heavily on her spirit. Yet, as the dust settled and she began to navigate her new reality, Vanessa discovered a profound strength within herself. This journey, though fraught with challenges, became a tapestry woven with moments of resilience and celebration. Small victories that illuminated her path.

The first small victory came when Vanessa managed to finish a book she had been reading before her diagnosis. It may seem trivial to some, but for her, it was a reminder of the life she had lived before cancer entered the picture. As she turned the last page, she felt a rush of accomplishment that brought a smile to her face. It was a moment of normalcy amidst the chaos, a fleeting escape into worlds crafted by words, offering her solace and hope.

Another significant milestone for Vanessa was her ability to take a short walk in the park near her home. Initially, the thought of physical exertion was daunting. The fatigue from treatments was often overwhelming, and her body felt foreign and heavy. However, one sunny afternoon, she mustered the courage to step outside. With each step, she inhaled the fresh air deeply, feeling the warmth of the sun on her skin. That short stroll became a symbol of her determination to reclaim her life, even if just for a little while.

As weeks turned into months, Vanessa celebrated her ability to cook a simple meal. Cooking had always been one of her passions, and the sight of fresh vegetables and spices reminded her of the joy she found in creating. On good days, she would invite her family over and prepare her favorite dishes. The laughter that filled her kitchen and the warmth of shared meals became a beacon of hope, illuminating the shadows that cancer cast over her life.

Vanessa also found strength in her connections with others. She joined a support group for cancer patients, where she met individuals who shared similar struggles. The first time she spoke about her experiences, she felt a wave of liberation wash over her. Sharing her story and listening to others reminded her that she was not alone in this battle. Each interaction became a small victory, reinforcing the power of community and shared resilience.

With each passing treatment cycle, Vanessa learned to appreciate the moments of feeling well. The days when she had the energy to engage in her hobbies, painting, gardening, or simply enjoying a cup of tea, became cherished milestones. She began to document these moments in a journal, writing down her thoughts and feelings. This practice became a form of therapy, allowing her to reflect on her journey and celebrate her resilience, even on the hardest days.

One of the most profound victories came when Vanessa decided to accept her hair loss. The process of losing her hair was daunting, yet she chose to embrace it with grace. Inviting her friends over to try on wigs, they gathered in her living room, laughter and tears mingling in the air. As the last strands fell to the ground, she felt a sense of empowerment wash over her. It was a symbolic act of reclaiming her identity, transforming what could have been a moment of despair into one of celebration and solidarity.

In the midst of her treatments, Vanessa made a conscious effort to practice gratitude. Each night, she would list three things she was grateful for, no matter how small. Sometimes it was the taste of her favorite tea or the laughter of a loved one. Other times, it was simply the comfort of her bed. This ritual shifted her perspective, allowing her to focus on the beauty of the present moment rather than the weight of her diagnosis. It became a small victory that nurtured her spirit and fostered hope.

As Vanessa continued her journey, she became an advocate for kidney cancer awareness. Sharing her story publicly, she connected with others who had been touched by the disease. Each time she spoke at an event or wrote an article, she felt a sense of purpose and fulfillment. Her voice became a beacon of hope for others, proving that even in the face of adversity, one could inspire change and foster a sense of community.

Vanessa's relationships deepened as she learned to lean on her loved ones. She began to express her feelings more openly, and this vulnerability brought her closer to her family and friends. Celebrating milestones together, whether it was a birthday or a simple game night, became a cherished ritual. The laughter and love shared in those moments were victories in themselves, reaffirming the importance of connection and support during her fight.

Ultimately, Vanessa's journey through stage 4 kidney cancer taught her the value of celebrating small victories. Each moment of joy, each act of resilience, contributed to her overall strength and determination. She learned that life, even in its most challenging times, was filled with beauty and hope. Through those small victories, Vanessa found a renewed sense of purpose. She realized that even the simplest moments could bring profound joy, transforming her outlook on life. Each day became an opportunity to savor experiences that once felt mundane. Whether it was watching the sunrise with a cup of coffee in hand or savoring the laughter of children playing in the park, she began to immerse herself fully in the present. This awakening was a testament to her evolving mindset. A shift from fear and uncertainty to gratitude and appreciation.

As Vanessa's journey continued, she developed a ritual of self-care that became a cornerstone of her daily life. On days when treatments left her feeling drained, she would indulge in a warm bubble bath, complete with calming music and aromatic candles. This simple act of self-love became a sanctuary where she could unwind and reconnect with herself. Each bath felt like a small victory, a reminder that she was deserving of care and comfort despite the challenges she faced.

In her quest for healing, Vanessa also turned to creativity as an outlet. She began painting again, something she had neglected for years. The canvas became a space for expression, a medium through which she could channel her emotions. With each brushstroke, she felt a cathartic release, transforming her pain into art. The finished pieces, vibrant and full of life, filled her home with color and warmth, serving as constant reminders of her resilience and ability to create beauty even in adversity.

As the seasons changed, so did Vanessa's outlook on her diagnosis. She found solace in nature, often taking a book outside to read in the landscapes that surrounded her. The act of connecting with the earth, of witnessing the blossoming flowers and the changing leaves, reminded her of the cycles of life. It was a poignant metaphor for her own journey, one of transformation, growth, and the beauty that could emerge from struggle.

During one particularly challenging week, Vanessa received an unexpected letter from a stranger who had read her story online. The woman expressed how Vanessa's words had inspired her to find strength in her own battle with cancer. This connection, forged through shared experiences, became a pivotal moment for Vanessa. She realized that her journey was not just about her own fight but also about the impact she could have on others. This newfound understanding became yet another small victory, igniting her passion for advocacy and community support.

Encouraged by the responses she received, Vanessa decided to organize a local book exhibition showcasing her daughter's books and raising awareness for kidney cancer. The event was a labor of love, where she invited other survivors, and supporters to share their stories through books. The night of the exhibition was filled with laughter, tears, and a deep sense of connection. Seeing strangers gather to celebrate resilience through creativity felt like a monumental victory. One that transcended her personal struggles and fostered a sense of community.

In her efforts, Vanessa also began to collaborate with local organizations dedicated to cancer research. She organized workshops and community events, where participants could read books and learn about kidney health. Each event was a celebration of life, a way to educate and empower others while honoring those affected by the disease. Through these initiatives, Vanessa not only celebrated her victories but also inspired others to join the fight against cancer.

The journey through treatment was not without its challenges, and Vanessa had her share of difficult days. However, she learned to embrace those moments as part of her story. Each setback became a lesson in vulnerability and strength. In her journal, she began to write about the tough days, acknowledging the pain but also the lessons learned. This practice of reflection helped her process her emotions and reinforced her belief that even in struggle, there was room for growth and resilience.

As Vanessa approached a significant milestone in her treatment journey, a year since her diagnosis, she organized a gathering of friends and family to celebrate. It was a night filled with stories, laughter, and gratitude for the journey they had all shared. In that moment, surrounded by love and support, she felt an overwhelming sense of joy. The gathering was a powerful reminder that while the road had been fraught with challenges, it had also been illuminated with moments of beauty and connection.

In the end, Vanessa emerged from her experience not just as a survivor but as a beacon of hope for others. She had learned that celebrating small victories was not only about acknowledging her progress but also about fostering a sense of community and resilience. Each step she took, each moment of joy she embraced, contributed to a larger narrative of strength and perseverance. Vanessa's journey transformed her perspective, allowing her to see life through a lens of gratitude. One that illuminated the beauty that exists even in the face of adversity.

Vanessa knew that her journey was far from over, but she felt equipped to face whatever lay ahead. With her heart full of hope and her spirit unyielding, she continued to celebrate the small victories, knowing that they were the building blocks of her strength. Through her advocacy, creativity, and the love of her family.

Chapter Twenty Five

The Role of Faith and Spirituality

Vanessa's journey through cancer was not merely a medical battle; it became a profound spiritual awakening that transformed her understanding of faith and the divine. Initially, when she received her diagnosis, she was engulfed in fear and uncertainty. However, as the days turned into weeks of treatment, she found that her faith became a sanctuary where she could retreat from the chaos of her circumstances. This refuge in faith allowed her to process her emotions and confront the reality of her illness while holding onto a flicker of hope.

In the early stages of her diagnosis, Vanessa felt an overwhelming sense of isolation. The fear of the unknown loomed large, and she often questioned why this was happening to her. It was during these dark moments that she began to lean heavily on her spirituality. She turned to prayer, seeking solace and guidance. Slowly but surely, she discovered that her connection to God was not just a source of comfort but also a catalyst for resilience. Each prayer became a lifeline, pulling her through the toughest days and instilling a sense of purpose in her struggle.

As Vanessa navigated the grueling treatments, she found herself surrounded by a community of believers who uplifted her spirit. Their unwavering faith and support acted as a beacon of light in her life. She realized that faith was not a solitary journey; it was a collective experience that thrived in the bonds of community. Through shared prayers and stories of hope, Vanessa's faith grew not only in God but also in the power of human connection. This camaraderie reinforced her belief that she was not alone in her fight, and together, they could overcome any obstacle.

With each passing day, Vanessa began to witness what she believed were miracles unfolding around her. Small victories in her treatment, moments of unexpected joy, and the love that enveloped her became evidence of God's handiwork in her life. She learned to celebrate these miracles, recognizing them as manifestations of divine grace. This newfound perspective transformed her outlook; she began to see her cancer not just as a challenge but as an opportunity for growth and deeper understanding of her faith.

The emotional toll of cancer was immense, but Vanessa found that her spirituality provided her with the strength to face her fears head-on. She immersed herself in scripture, drawing inspiration from stories of resilience and faith in adversity. These narratives resonated deeply with her own journey, reminding her that others had walked similar paths and emerged stronger. Each verse became a source of empowerment, a reminder that her struggles were not in vain and that God was with her every step of the way.

As her treatment progressed, Vanessa experienced moments of profound clarity. In the quiet of her hospital room and during solitary moments of reflection, she felt a deep sense of peace wash over her. It was during these instances that she understood the true essence of faith: it was not about having all the answers but rather trusting in God's plan. This realization brought her comfort, allowing her to surrender her fears and embrace the uncertainty with grace and courage.

The act of gratitude became a cornerstone of Vanessa's spiritual journey. She started a daily practice of writing down things she was thankful for, no matter how small. This simple act shifted her focus from fear and despair to appreciation for the life she had and the love surrounding her. She expressed gratitude for her medical team, her supportive family, and even the lessons learned through her struggles. Each entry in her gratitude journal became a testament to God's presence in her life, reinforcing her belief in the miracles that were unfolding.

As she moved toward recovery, Vanessa's faith transformed from a means of survival into a vibrant part of her identity. She began to share her story, speaking at local churches and support groups, inspiring others with her journey of faith through adversity. Vanessa understood that her experience was not just for her own healing but also a way to uplift others facing similar challenges. She became a living testament to the power of faith, demonstrating how it could carry one through the darkest valleys and into the light.

Emerging victorious from her battle with cancer, Vanessa felt an overwhelming sense of gratitude for the journey. She recognized that her experiences had deepened her relationship with God and strengthened her resolve to live a life of purpose. With a renewed spirit, she committed herself to helping others navigate their own struggles, offering support and encouragement. Her faith was no longer a passive belief but an active force that inspired her to make a difference in the world.

Vanessa's journey taught her that faith is a dynamic process, continually evolving as one faces life's challenges. The trials she endured became a crucible for her spirituality, refining her beliefs and enriching her understanding of God's love. She emerged not just as a survivor of cancer but as a beacon of hope for others, embodying the message that faith can transform suffering into strength and despair into gratitude. Her story is a beautiful reminder of the miracles that unfold when one places their trust in a higher power.

In the end, Vanessa's life became a testimony to the power of faith that transcends mere belief; it became a living expression of resilience, hope, and love. She learned that faith is not just a passive acceptance of circumstances but an active engagement with life's challenges. Each setback became an opportunity for growth, and each triumph was a reminder of the divine presence guiding her journey. With every step forward, she recognized that her experience was not just about her individual struggle, but part of a larger tapestry of human experience.

Vanessa's newfound purpose extended beyond her own recovery. Inspired by her transformative journey, she began volunteering at local cancer support organizations, where she could share her story and offer encouragement to those who were just beginning their battles. She often found herself in deep conversations with patients who were frightened and uncertain, just as she once was. Through these interactions, she not only provided comfort but also learned from their stories, realizing that the human spirit is incredibly resilient, often in ways we cannot yet understand.

In her volunteer work, Vanessa also discovered the importance of community in the healing process. She organized support groups, creating safe spaces for individuals to share their feelings, fears, and hopes. These gatherings became a sanctuary where faith, love, and compassion flourished. Vanessa saw firsthand the power of collective prayer and mutual support, reinforcing her belief that together, we can uplift one another in our darkest times. The bonds formed in those groups became a testament to the strength of community and the divine connections that exist among us.

As her role in the community expanded, Vanessa also took the opportunity to explore her spirituality more deeply. She began attending retreats and workshops focused on faith and healing, where she delved into practices like meditation and mindfulness. These experiences enriched her spiritual life, allowing her to connect with God in new and profound ways. She found that through quiet reflection and stillness, she could tap into an inner reservoir of strength and serenity that had always been there, waiting to be discovered.

Throughout her journey, Vanessa remained profoundly aware of the miracles that had occurred in her life. She often reflected on the small yet significant moments, like the kindness of strangers, the laughter shared with friends, and the beauty of nature, that had helped sustain her spirit. These moments became markers of her faith, reminders that God's love is often expressed through the people and experiences that surround us. Her heart swelled with gratitude as she realized that even in pain, blessings could be found.

Embracing her identity as a survivor, Vanessa also felt called to advocate for cancer awareness and research. She began participating in fundraising events, using her voice to raise awareness about the importance of early detection and the need for continued support for those affected by cancer. Her advocacy was not just about her own experience, but about ensuring that others had access to the resources and support they needed. Vanessa's faith fueled her passion, driving her to be a beacon of hope within her community and beyond.

In her personal life, Vanessa's relationships flourished as well. The experience of battling cancer brought her closer to her loved ones, deepening their connections and fostering a sense of unity. She often expressed her gratitude to her family and friends, acknowledging their unwavering support during her darkest days. This sense of gratitude spilled over into all areas of her life, transforming her interactions into opportunities for love and connection. Each day became a gift, and she cherished the moments spent with those she held dear.

As Vanessa continued to grow in her faith, she also found that her perspective on life had shifted dramatically. She no longer took the small things for granted; every sunrise was a reminder of renewal, and every moment spent with loved ones was a treasure. She learned to appreciate the beauty in imperfection, understanding that life's unpredictability is part of the divine plan. This newfound appreciation for life propelled her to live with intentionality, pursuing her passions and savoring every experience.

Vanessa's journey was not without its challenges, but she faced each obstacle with a spirit fortified by faith. She learned to navigate life's uncertainties with grace, trusting that God was at work in her life even when the path seemed unclear. Her faith became a compass, guiding her through the storms and reminding her of the hope that lay on the other side. Each challenge reinforced her belief in the resilience of the human spirit and the power of divine love.

Ultimately, Vanessa emerged from her cancer journey not just as a survivor but as a warrior of faith. She had learned that faith is not a destination but a journey. One that requires continual nurturing, reflection, and growth. Her experience had shaped her into a compassionate advocate, a loving friend, and a source of inspiration for others. As she looked toward the future, Vanessa carried with her the lessons learned and the miracles witnessed, ready to embrace whatever lay ahead with an open heart and unwavering faith.

In sharing her story, Vanessa became a beacon of hope, embodying the belief that even in the face of adversity, we can find strength, purpose, and the extraordinary hand of God guiding us.

Chapter Twenty Six

Family Bonds Strengthened

Vanessa had always believed that family was the cornerstone of her existence. Growing up in a small town, she was surrounded by the warmth of her parents and family. Each family member played a vital role in shaping her values, beliefs, and emotional resilience. The bonds they shared were built on trust, love, and unwavering support. As Vanessa transitioned into adulthood, these connections became even more significant, reinforcing the idea that family was not just about blood but about the relationships nurtured over time.

One of the defining moments that strengthened Vanessa's family ties came during a challenging period when her mother fell ill. The news was devastating, and the family quickly rallied together. They took turns caring for her, ensuring she had everything she needed. This experience brought them closer as they shared their fears, hopes, and frustrations. Vanessa realized that adversity often has a way of illuminating the strength of familial bonds, and through this trial, her family emerged more united than ever.

The family, once caught up in their own lives, found themselves reconnecting in ways they hadn't anticipated. They began hosting weekly family dinners, where they would share stories, laughter, and even tears. These gatherings became a haven for them, a space where they could express their feelings and support one another. Vanessa noticed how these simple acts of coming together created a deeper understanding among them, reinforcing their commitment to one another and the importance of family in their lives.

As time passed, the family dynamics evolved, and Vanessa took on a more proactive role in maintaining their bonds. She organized family outings, game nights, and even weekend retreats. Each event served as a reminder of the joy that comes from being together. Vanessa found immense satisfaction in seeing her family members connect and enjoy each other's company. These moments were not just about fun but about building a legacy of love and support that would endure through the years.

The strength of Vanessa's family bonds was further tested when her older brother faced a significant life challenge. Struggling with career decisions and personal setbacks, he felt lost and overwhelmed. Vanessa, recognizing his struggles, stepped in to provide guidance and encouragement. Their late-night conversations, filled with laughter and tears, became a lifeline for him. In supporting her brother, Vanessa discovered the depth of her own resilience and the profound impact that familial love can have in times of crisis.

As the family continued to navigate life's ups and downs, they learned to communicate more openly. They established a tradition of monthly family meetings where everyone could voice their thoughts and feelings. This practice not only enhanced their understanding of each other but also created a safe space for addressing conflicts and concerns. Vanessa felt empowered by the newfound openness, knowing that they were all committed to fostering a supportive environment where everyone's voice mattered.

The bonds within Vanessa's family were also strengthened through shared experiences. They embarked on a family vacation that had been long overdue, exploring new destinations and creating cherished memories. The trip was filled with laughter, adventure, and moments of reflection. It served as a reminder of the importance of taking time out of their busy lives to reconnect and appreciate each other. Vanessa realized that these experiences were crucial in solidifying their relationships and creating a sense of belonging.

As the years went by, Vanessa became increasingly aware of the importance of legacy. She wanted to ensure that the values of love, support, and togetherness were passed down to future generations. With this in mind, she began documenting their family stories, creating a scrapbook filled with photographs, anecdotes, and lessons learned. This project became a labor of love, allowing her to reflect on their journey while also giving her family a tangible reminder of their strength and resilience.

In moments of reflection, Vanessa often thought about how far they had come as a family. The challenges they had faced had only served to deepen their bonds, and she felt grateful for the lessons learned along the way. The love they shared was a testament to their commitment to one another, and she cherished the knowledge that they would always be there for each other, no matter what life threw their way. The strength of their family ties was a powerful reminder that love is not merely a feeling but a choice made every day.

As she moved forward in life, Vanessa understood that family bonds require nurturing and attention. She made it a point to prioritize her relationships, ensuring that they remained strong and vibrant. Whether through small gestures, heartfelt conversations, or simply being present, she dedicated herself to maintaining the connections that had brought her so much joy and strength. Vanessa knew that, in the end, it was these relationships that would sustain her through life's challenges.

Ultimately, the journey of strengthening family bonds had transformed Vanessa's life. It taught her the value of resilience, the power of love, and the importance of being there for one another. She felt an unbreakable connection with her family, one that would endure through the trials and triumphs of life. As she looked toward the future, Vanessa was filled with hope and determination, knowing that no matter As Vanessa continued to reflect on the importance of family, she recognized that their bonds were not just formed through shared experiences but also through the challenges they had overcome together. Each obstacle had become a thread in the tapestry of their family story, weaving a narrative of resilience and unity. These shared challenges taught her that adversity was not something to be feared but embraced as an opportunity for growth. The lessons learned during difficult times became a source of strength, reminding them all of the power found in sticking together.

During one family gathering, Vanessa decided to share her thoughts on their journey. She expressed her gratitude for each family member, emphasizing how their unique qualities contributed to the family dynamic. Her heartfelt words resonated deeply, and the room filled with emotion as they collectively acknowledged the strength they had found in one another. This moment of vulnerability deepened their connections, reinforcing the idea that expressing love and appreciation was just as crucial as the support they provided during tough times.

As Vanessa took on the role of family historian, she began to encourage each member to share their own stories and experiences. She organized storytelling nights, where they would gather around a cozy fire, sharing tales from their past, both humorous and poignant. These sessions became a treasured tradition, creating a sense of belonging and continuity. It allowed them to see how their individual journeys were interwoven, deepening their understanding of each other's lives and perspectives.

The importance of family traditions also became apparent to Vanessa. She initiated new rituals, such as a yearly family reunion and a dedicated day for volunteering together. These traditions not only provided structure to their gatherings but also fostered a sense of purpose. Giving back to the community collectively reinforced their bonds and instilled a shared sense of responsibility and gratitude. Vanessa realized that the act of serving others brought them closer together and enriched their own lives in the process.

As Vanessa nurtured her family connections, she also recognized the importance of setting boundaries. While it was essential to be there for each other, it was equally vital to respect individual needs and personal space. This balance allowed them to maintain healthy relationships and fostered a sense of independence within the family unit. Vanessa found that open discussions about boundaries only strengthened their ties, as it showed a level of respect and understanding that deepened their connections.

The passage of time brought changes to the family dynamics, with siblings marrying and starting families of their own. Vanessa embraced these changes with open arms, understanding that growth was a natural part of life. She welcomed new members into their fold, seeing them as opportunities to expand their family bonds. Each new addition brought fresh perspectives and unique experiences, enriching their collective narrative and reinforcing the idea that family is ever-evolving.

Through these transformations, Vanessa remained committed to creating a legacy of love and support. She actively engaged with her nieces and nephews, wanting to instill in them the same values that had been passed down to her. Vanessa organized activities and educational outings, emphasizing the importance of family history and connection. She hoped to inspire the younger generation to cherish their familial bonds and understand the strength that comes from unity.

In her heart, Vanessa knew that the foundation she had helped build would endure. The strength of their family bonds was a beacon of hope and reassurance, guiding them through whatever life had in store. As she looked ahead, she felt a profound sense of peace knowing that no matter how far apart they might be or what challenges they faced, their love for one another would always remain a constant source of strength. The story of their family was one of resilience, unity, and unwavering support. A legacy that would continue to flourish for generations to come.

Chapter Twenty Seven

The Gift of Perspective

Vanessa had a unique ability to see the world through a lens that few could access. This gift of perspective allowed her to navigate life's complexities with a grace that often left those around her in awe. It wasn't merely about empathy or understanding; it was a profound insight that enabled her to view situations from multiple angles, recognizing the subtleties that others might overlook. Friends often joked that she had a sixth sense, one that allowed her to read the room and the emotions of people within it.

Growing up in a diverse neighborhood, Vanessa was exposed to a plethora of cultures, beliefs, and experiences. Her childhood was a mosaic of interactions that shaped her worldview. She learned early on that each person had a story, a history that influenced their actions and reactions. This insight fostered her ability to connect with others on a deeper level, as she understood that everyone carried their own burdens, joys, and fears. Vanessa's perspective was rooted in this understanding of shared humanity, allowing her to approach conversations with patience and compassion.

As she entered adulthood, Vanessa's gift evolved into a tool for conflict resolution. Friends and colleagues often turned to her when tensions rose, knowing that she could help untangle the knots of miscommunication. In a workplace fraught with competition and ambition, her ability to see both sides of an argument brought clarity to heated discussions. She would often ask questions that prompted others to think beyond their initial reactions, encouraging a dialogue that fostered understanding rather than division. Vanessa became known as the peacemaker, a title she wore with humility.

However, Vanessa's perspective was not always welcomed. Some found her insights uncomfortable, especially when they challenged long-held beliefs. In a world that often favors conformity, her ability to question the status quo made her a target for criticism. Yet, Vanessa remained undeterred. She believed that growth often came from discomfort, and she wasn't afraid to confront difficult truths. Her friends admired her courage, even if they occasionally found themselves defensive when faced with her probing questions.

In her personal life, Vanessa's gift allowed her to cultivate deep and meaningful relationships. She had an uncanny knack for making people feel seen and heard, which drew friends and strangers alike into her orbit. During moments of crisis, people would seek her out for guidance, knowing that she would not only listen but also help them reframe their problems. This transformative ability to shift perspective was akin to offering a new pair of glasses to someone who had been squinting at the world for too long.

Vanessa's perspective also enriched her creative endeavors. As an artist, she infused her work with the stories she encountered, translating them into visual narratives that resonated with a broad audience. Her paintings often depicted scenes of everyday life, yet they were imbued with layers of meaning that invited viewers to engage with their own experiences. Critics praised her ability to capture the essence of humanity, and her exhibitions became spaces for reflection and conversation.

Yet, with such a gift came the burden of constant observation. Vanessa often found herself overwhelmed by the emotions and energies of those around her. This sensitivity was a double-edged sword; while it enriched her understanding, it also drained her. She learned the importance of setting boundaries, recognizing that her gift required self-care. Meditation and nature walks became her sanctuaries, places where she could recharge and reconnect with her own perspective, free from the weight of others' emotions.

In moments of solitude, Vanessa reflected on her journey and the responsibility that came with her gift. She understood that her perspective was not infallible; it was shaped by her own experiences and biases. This awareness fueled her desire to continue learning and growing, to broaden her lens rather than narrow it. She read voraciously, engaged in discussions, and sought out experiences that challenged her views, determined to remain open and adaptable.

As Vanessa continued to navigate life's complexities, she became a mentor to others seeking to develop their own perspectives. She hosted workshops and discussions, encouraging participants to explore their beliefs and assumptions. Through storytelling and shared experiences, Vanessa created a safe space for others to embrace vulnerability and growth. Her commitment to fostering perspective in others was a testament to her belief in the transformative power of understanding.

In a world that often feels polarized and fragmented, Vanessa's gift of perspective shone like a beacon of hope. She embodied the idea that change begins with understanding, and that empathy can bridge even the widest divides. Her life's work became a celebration of diversity, a reminder that every individual's story adds richness to the tapestry of humanity. Vanessa's legacy was not just in the insights she shared but in the lives she touched, inspiring others to embrace their own gifts of perspective.

Ultimately, Vanessa understood that her gift was a journey rather than a destination. Each encounter, each conversation, shaped her understanding of the world and her place within it. As she continued to evolve, she remained committed to the idea that perspective was a

As Vanessa navigated her journey, she became increasingly aware of the interconnectedness of all things. The threads of individual stories began to weave together, forming a rich tapestry of human experience. This realization deepened her appreciation for the beauty that lay in diversity. She found joy in exploring how different backgrounds, cultures, and lived experiences shaped perspectives. Vanessa often organized community events that celebrated this diversity, bringing people together to share their stories through art, music, and conversation, further reinforcing her belief in the power of perspective.

One day, while in a discussion group, Vanessa encountered a particularly challenging situation. A participant voiced strong opinions that clashed with the views of others, creating an atmosphere of tension. Instead of shying away from the discomfort, Vanessa chose to step into the fray. She gently encouraged the individual to articulate their thoughts while inviting others to share their counterarguments. This delicate dance of dialogue illuminated the nuances of the debate, revealing common ground that had previously been obscured. Vanessa's ability to mediate such discussions reinforced her role as a facilitator of understanding.

Vanessa's gift also extended into her family life. She often found herself playing the role of the mediator during family gatherings, where differing opinions could sometimes spark heated arguments. By employing her characteristic patience, she helped family members see each other's viewpoints, facilitating conversations that led to deeper connections. This role was not without its challenges, as she sometimes felt the weight of her family's expectations. Still, she took pride in her ability to foster unity, ensuring that love and understanding prevailed over division.

In her romantic relationships, Vanessa's perspective was both a blessing and a challenge. Her partners often appreciated her ability to understand their feelings deeply, yet this same sensitivity could lead to misunderstandings. She learned that while it was essential to empathize, it was equally vital to communicate her own needs and boundaries. Through open conversations, she cultivated relationships based on mutual respect and understanding, continually refining her ability to balance her gift with the reality of her own emotional landscape.

As Vanessa's reputation as a perspective-shifter grew, she received invitations to speak at various conferences and workshops. These opportunities allowed her to share her insights with a broader audience, empowering others to embrace their own abilities to see the world through different lenses. She spoke passionately about the importance of perspective in leadership, collaboration, and personal growth, emphasizing that understanding diverse viewpoints could lead to innovative solutions in both personal and professional realms.

Yet, public speaking also introduced new challenges. With each event, Vanessa faced the pressure of expectation. Would her insights resonate? Would she be able to convey the depth of her understanding adequately? These doubts sometimes crept into her mind, threatening to overshadow her confidence. However, she quickly learned to transform this anxiety into motivation, seeing each opportunity as a chance to grow and connect. With every speech, she became more attuned to the audience's energy, using it to refine her message and deepen the impact of her words.

As she continued to develop her skills, Vanessa sought out mentors who had navigated similar paths. She engaged with authors, psychologists, and public figures who had made their mark by fostering understanding across divides. These interactions inspired her to think critically about her own journey, prompting her to question her assumptions and expand her horizons. Vanessa realized that learning was a lifelong process, and she embraced this idea wholeheartedly, knowing it would enrich her perspective even further.

One particularly transformative experience came when Vanessa traveled abroad for a cultural exchange program. Immersed in a different environment, she was struck by the stark contrasts in daily life and customs. Yet, rather than seeing these differences as barriers, she viewed them as windows into another world. Each conversation she had with locals opened her eyes to new ways of thinking and being. This journey reinforced her belief that perspective was not only about understanding others but also about embracing the unfamiliar with curiosity and openness.

Upon returning home, Vanessa felt a renewed sense of purpose. She began to integrate her experiences into her art, using her creative outlets to express the rich tapestry of perspectives she had encountered. Each brushstroke told a story of connection, of bridging gaps between cultures and experiences. Her exhibitions took on a new depth, resonating with audiences on an emotional level, encouraging them to reflect on their own perspectives and experiences. Art, she realized, was a powerful medium for fostering understanding and dialogue.

As Vanessa continued to share her gift, she became increasingly aware of the responsibilities that came with it. She recognized the importance of humility and continuous learning, understanding that no one person could hold all the answers. This realization grounded her, reminding her that the journey of perspective was ever-evolving. It was a dance of listening and sharing, questioning and affirming, and it required her to remain open to change. In the end, Vanessa's journey was a testament to the transformative power of perspective.

Chapter Twenty Eight

Inspiring Others: Sharing My Story

Vanessa's journey with stage four kidney cancer began with a routine check-up that turned into a life-altering diagnosis. She found herself grappling with an overwhelming flood of emotions, fear, confusion, and disbelief. However, as the reality of her situation sunk in, Vanessa realized that she had an opportunity to share her story and inspire others facing their own challenges. Rather than retreating into despair, she chose to embrace her circumstances and use her experience as a platform to uplift those around her.

From the moment Vanessa shared her diagnosis with friends and family, she was met with an outpouring of love and support. Instead of allowing her illness to isolate her, she opened her heart and home to those who wanted to be part of her journey. Vanessa began hosting regular gatherings where she would discuss not only her treatment plans but also the emotional and psychological turmoil that accompanied her diagnosis. These gatherings became a sanctuary for others, offering a space for vulnerability and connection, as she encouraged her loved ones to express their fears and hopes.

Vanessa's approach to her treatment was both proactive and positive. She began documenting her experiences, sharing the highs and lows of her journey. Her candid posts about chemotherapy sessions, the side effects, and the moments of despair resonated with many. She used her platform to educate others about kidney cancer, advocating for awareness and early detection. Vanessa's transparency about her struggles and triumphs made her followers feel seen and understood, fostering a sense of community among those who were also battling cancer or supporting loved ones through their own journeys.

In the face of adversity, Vanessa discovered a newfound strength within herself. She began participating in local cancer support groups, where she not only found solace but also the opportunity to help others navigate their own paths. Listening to the stories of others battling cancer ignited a fire within her, compelling her to take action. Vanessa organized workshops that focused on coping mechanisms, mindfulness, and the importance of mental health during a cancer diagnosis. She became a beacon of hope, reminding others that they were not alone and that it was possible to find joy even in the darkest of times.

As Vanessa continued to share her journey, she began to receive messages from strangers who were inspired by her resilience. Individuals from all walks of life reached out to thank her for her honesty and encouragement. Vanessa realized that her story was reaching beyond her immediate circle, touching lives in ways she had never anticipated. This realization propelled her to speak at cancer awareness events and support groups, where she shared her story with larger audiences. Her ability to connect with people on a personal level resonated deeply, inspiring them to face their own battles with courage.

One of the most profound impacts of Vanessa's journey was the way it fostered empathy and connection among those who attended the events. People began to share their own stories, creating a tapestry of experiences that highlighted the resilience of the human spirit. Vanessa encouraged these conversations, emphasizing that vulnerability is a strength, not a weakness. By creating an environment where sharing was welcomed, she helped individuals find their voices and reclaim their narratives, empowering them to take charge of their healing journeys.

Vanessa's advocacy extended beyond her personal experiences. She became actively involved in reasearch efforts for kidney cancer research, channeling her energy into initiatives that aimed to make a difference for future patients.

Vanessa's commitment to improving the lives of others showcased her selflessness and reminded everyone that even in the face of personal challenges, one can contribute to the greater good.

Through her journey, Vanessa also discovered the importance of self-care and balance. She began sharing tips on how to maintain a positive mindset, incorporating activities like yoga, meditation, and journaling into her routine. Her followers were inspired by her dedication to nurturing her mental and emotional well-being, realizing that these practices were vital components of their own journeys. Vanessa's willingness to embrace self-care became a rallying cry for others, encouraging them to prioritize their well-being amidst the chaos of life.

As Vanessa's story continued to unfold, she became a symbol of hope and resilience. The impact of her journey reached far and wide, as people began to share her posts and spread her message of courage. Vanessa's authenticity and vulnerability resonated deeply, inspiring countless individuals to advocate for their health, seek support, and find strength in community. She demonstrated that while cancer is a formidable opponent, it does not define one's identity or diminish one's capacity for joy and connection.

Ultimately, Vanessa's journey with stage four kidney cancer became a testament to the power of storytelling and the human spirit. She inspired others to embrace their struggles, to find purpose in their pain, and to recognize the strength that lies within. Through her unwavering determination to share her experiences, Vanessa transformed her journey into a source of inspiration for many, proving that even in the face of life's greatest challenges.

Vanessa's journey was not without its challenges, and she faced moments of profound despair. There were days when the weight of her diagnosis felt unbearable, and the thought of her mortality loomed large. During these tough times, she leaned on her support system—the friends and family who had rallied around her since the beginning. They became a source of strength, reminding her of the love and connection that persisted even in the darkest moments. Vanessa learned the importance of asking for help and recognized that vulnerability could be a source of strength rather than a sign of weakness.

Inspired by the support she received, Vanessa initiated a "cancer buddy" program, pairing newly diagnosed patients with those who had been through similar experiences. This initiative created a network of support, allowing individuals to share their fears, hopes, and practical advice on navigating treatment. Vanessa's compassionate approach helped foster meaningful connections, reassuring others that they were not alone on their journey. The program grew rapidly, with participants expressing gratitude for the sense of community it provided during their most challenging moments.

As Vanessa became more involved in her advocacy, she was invited to speak at various conferences and seminars. Each opportunity allowed her to share her message of hope and resilience with larger audiences. Her authenticity shone through as she recounted her experiences, weaving together stories of struggle and triumph. Vanessa often emphasized the need for a holistic approach to cancer treatment, one that acknowledges the emotional and psychological aspects of the journey. Her insights resonated with both patients and healthcare professionals, sparking discussions about the importance of mental health in cancer care.

In her quest to inspire others, Vanessa also began collaborating with local artists to create a series of artworks that depicted her journey. These pieces captured not only the physical challenges of her illness but also the emotional landscape of her experience. Through visual storytelling, Vanessa aimed to convey the beauty that can coexist with pain and to inspire hope in others. The art installations were showcased in community centers, sparking conversations about cancer, resilience, and the power of creative expression in healing.

As Vanessa's platform grew, she advocated for other cancer survivors, healthcare and professionals. Each episode delved into the intricacies of living with cancer, exploring topics such as nutrition, mental health, and the importance of community support. Vanessa's genuine curiosity and empathy created a safe space for her guests to share their stories, allowing listeners to gain insights and practical advice. The platform became a valuable resource for those seeking inspiration and guidance, further extending Vanessa's reach and impact.

Recognizing the need for accessible resources, Vanessa organized to develop informational materials for patients and caregivers. These resources included guides on navigating treatment options, understanding side effects, and finding emotional support. By providing practical tools, Vanessa aimed to empower individuals to take charge of their health and advocate for themselves within the healthcare system. Her commitment to education not only benefited those directly affected by cancer but also raised awareness among the general public.

Despite her busy schedule, Vanessa prioritized self-care, understanding its critical role in her well-being. She regularly practiced mindfulness, yoga, and journaling, sharing her routines with her followers to inspire them to carve out time for themselves. Vanessa emphasized that self-care was not a luxury but a necessity, especially for those facing health challenges. Her openness about her own struggles with self-care served as a reminder that it was okay to have ups and downs, and that seeking balance was a continuous journey.

Over time, Vanessa's advocacy efforts began to gain recognition within her community and beyond. She received awards for her contributions to cancer awareness and patient support, but she remained humble, always redirecting the spotlight to the stories of others. Vanessa believed that her role was to amplify voices that often went unheard in the cancer community. She understood that by sharing the experiences of others, she could continue to inspire hope and resilience in the face of adversity.

As her journey progressed, Vanessa faced the reality of her illness with grace and strength. She often reflected on her life, cherishing the moments of joy and connection that had emerged from her diagnosis. She organized "celebration days" to honor milestones in her treatment journey, inviting friends and family to join her in celebrating life. These gatherings served as a testament to her belief that even amidst the struggle, life was worth celebrating. Vanessa's ability to find joy in the little things became a guiding principle for those who walked alongside her.

In her final chapters, Vanessa emphasized the importance of legacy and the impact one can leave on the world. She encouraged her followers to live authentically, pursue their passions, and cherish their relationships. She often reminded them that each person has a unique story that can inspire others, regardless of the challenges they face. Vanessa's unwavering spirit and commitment to sharing her journey became a lasting testament to the resilience of the human spirit, a reminder that hope can thrive even in the face of the greatest obstacles.

Chapter Twenty Nine

Reclaiming Joy in Everyday Life

Vanessa was once a vibrant soul, known for her laughter and zest for life. However, when she was diagnosed with stage four kidney cancer, everything changed. The news felt like a dark cloud hanging over her, casting shadows on her dreams and aspirations. Initially, she was engulfed in fear and uncertainty, struggling to come to terms with her diagnosis. The physical pain and emotional toll weighed heavily on her spirit, and joy became a distant memory, overshadowed by hospital visits, treatments, and the omnipresent fear of the unknown.

As the treatments progressed, Vanessa found herself at a crossroads. She could either surrender to despair or fight to reclaim her joy amidst the chaos. With a determined heart, she chose the latter. It wasn't an easy path, but she began to seek out small moments of happiness in her daily life. She started to appreciate the little things. A warm cup of tea on a chilly morning, the sound of birds chirping outside her window, or the way the sunlight streamed through her curtains. These seemingly trivial moments began to stitch threads of joy back into the fabric of her life.

Realizing that joy could coexist with her illness, Vanessa began to curate her environment to nurture positivity. She filled her space with photographs of loved ones, reminders of joyful memories, and inspirational quotes that resonated with her spirit. She decorated her room with vibrant colors that uplifted her mood and created a sanctuary where she could escape the weight of her diagnosis. This intentional curation of her surroundings became a powerful tool in her journey to reclaiming joy, allowing her to focus on what truly mattered amidst the challenges she faced.

In her quest for joy, Vanessa also turned to creativity as a form of expression and healing. She picked up her paintbrush again, something she hadn't done in years, and let her emotions flow onto the canvas. Each stroke became a cathartic release, transforming her pain into art. She found solace in colors, shapes, and the act of creation, allowing herself to express feelings that were often too complex for words. This rediscovery of her passion for painting not only provided a creative outlet but also a sense of accomplishment and hope.

Connecting with others became another vital aspect of Vanessa's journey. She reached out to friends and family, sharing her experiences and allowing them to support her in her battle. The conversations ranged from deep and meaningful to light-hearted and silly, reminding her of the beauty of human connection. She also joined a support group for cancer patients, where she met others who were navigating similar challenges. Sharing stories and laughter with those who understood her journey brought an unexpected joy that filled her heart with warmth.

Mindfulness and gratitude practices emerged as essential tools for Vanessa in her daily life. Each morning, she began to write down three things she was grateful for, no matter how small. This practice shifted her perspective, allowing her to focus on the positive aspects of her life rather than solely on her illness. Meditation became a refuge, offering her moments of peace and clarity. Through mindfulness, Vanessa learned to embrace the present, finding joy in the simple act of being alive, even on difficult days.

As her journey continued, Vanessa discovered the healing power of nature. She began taking short walks in her neighborhood, soaking in the beauty of blooming flowers, rustling leaves, and the gentle breeze. The fresh air invigorated her spirit, and she found herself captivated by the colors and sounds of the world around her. Nature became a source of inspiration, reminding her of the resilience of life. These walks transformed into moments of reflection, where she could breathe deeply and appreciate the gift of each day.

Vanessa also made it a priority to indulge in experiences that brought her joy. She returned to her love for music, attending concerts and listening to her favorite albums, allowing the melodies to uplift her spirits. She hosted small gatherings with friends, filling her home with laughter and love. Each shared meal, each heartfelt conversation, and each moment of connection reminded her that joy could thrive even in the face of adversity. These experiences created a tapestry of memories that became a source of strength for her.

Through her journey, Vanessa learned the importance of self-compassion. There were days when she felt overwhelmed and exhausted, and she realized that it was okay to not always be strong. Embracing her vulnerability allowed her to navigate the emotional complexities of her illness. She began to practice self-care, whether it was taking a long bath, reading a captivating book, or simply allowing herself to rest without guilt. This nurturing of her own spirit became a crucial element in her reclamation of joy.

As Vanessa continued to embrace joy in her everyday life, she became an inspiration to those around her. Her story of resilience and hope spread, touching the hearts of friends, family, and even strangers. She used her platform to advocate for awareness about kidney cancer and the importance of living fully, even in the face of challenges. Vanessa's journey became a testament to the fact that joy

could be found even in the darkest of times. She shared her insights through social media, connecting with a larger community of individuals facing similar battles. Her authenticity resonated with many, and she quickly became a beacon of hope for those grappling with their own struggles. Each post was a reminder that life, despite its trials, could still be filled with moments of light and laughter.

One day, inspired by the positive response she received, Vanessa decided to host an art exhibit showcasing her paintings alongside stories of her journey. She titled it "Colors of Resilience," inviting friends, family, and even members of her support group to contribute their own stories of struggle and triumph. The event was a celebration of life, love, and the indomitable spirit of those facing cancer. As she stood amid the vibrant canvases and heartfelt narratives, she felt a profound connection to each person present, reinforcing her belief that joy is often found in shared experiences.

With each passing day, Vanessa embraced her new reality, recognizing that while cancer had changed her life, it did not define her. She began to see her diagnosis as a catalyst for growth and transformation. It pushed her to prioritize what truly mattered: relationships, experiences, and the pursuit of happiness. No longer anchored by fear, she ventured into new hobbies, like gardening. Planting seeds and watching them flourish became a metaphor for her journey—an act of nurturing life even when faced with uncertainty.

Her relationship with her family deepened as they navigated this journey together. They started a weekly tradition of "Joyful Sundays," where they would gather for brunch, play games, and share their favorite memories. These gatherings transformed into a sanctuary of laughter and love, allowing them to create new memories while honoring the challenges they faced. Vanessa realized that the joy she reclaimed was not just for herself; it was a collective experience that strengthened the bonds within her family.

Vanessa also discovered the therapeutic benefits of volunteering. She began working with local organizations focused on cancer awareness and support, sharing her story to empower others. Engaging with the community brought her immense joy, as she witnessed the impact of her words and actions on those around her. It became a source of purpose, reminding her that she could still make a difference in the lives of others, even while navigating her own battles.

As her journey continued, Vanessa learned to celebrate milestones, both big and small. Whether it was completing a round of treatment or simply enjoying a day free from pain, she made it a point to acknowledge her victories. She treated herself to small rewards—like a new book, a spa day, or a weekend getaway with friends. Each celebration became a reminder that joy could be found in the journey, and it was essential to honor her progress, no matter how minor it seemed.

In her quest for joy, Vanessa also became an advocate for holistic health practices. She explored yoga, mindfulness, and nutrition, recognizing the power of self-care in her overall well-being. These practices not only helped her manage the physical and emotional aspects of her illness but also cultivated a deeper sense of connection to herself. She discovered that caring for her body and mind was an essential part of reclaiming joy, empowering her to face each day with renewed strength.

Through all the ups and downs, Vanessa's story became one of hope and resilience. Her journey was not without its challenges, but she learned to navigate the complexities with grace and courage. She understood that joy was not a constant state but rather a series of moments to be cherished. Each day brought new opportunities to find happiness, whether it was through a shared laugh, a quiet moment of reflection, or the warmth of the sun on her face.

Ultimately, Vanessa emerged from her battle with stage four kidney cancer not just as a survivor but as a warrior of joy. She embraced life with open arms, knowing that while her journey was shaped by her diagnosis, it was her spirit, love, and laughter that truly defined her existence. By reclaiming joy in her everyday life, she transformed her experience into a powerful narrative of hope, inspiring others to seek their own moments of happiness, no matter the circumstances they face. Vanessa's legacy became a testament to the enduring power of the human spirit, a reminder that joy can bloom even in the harshest of environments.

Chapter Thirty

Self Advocacy and Awareness

Vanessa's journey with stage four kidney cancer has been a profound testament to self-advocacy and awareness. Initially diagnosed with renal cell carcinoma, she faced a whirlwind of emotions—fear, confusion, and the overwhelming weight of uncertainty. However, rather than succumbing to despair, Vanessa chose to take control of her narrative. She immersed herself in research, learning everything she could about her condition, treatment options, and the latest advancements in oncology. This proactive approach not only empowered her but also equipped her with the knowledge necessary to navigate the complex healthcare system.

From the outset, Vanessa recognized the importance of communication in her advocacy. She began to articulate her symptoms, concerns, and treatment preferences with clarity and confidence. This open dialogue with her medical team fostered a collaborative environment, allowing her to feel more involved in her care decisions. Vanessa understood that being an active participant in her treatment was crucial; it was not merely about following a prescribed path but about tailoring her journey to her unique needs and circumstances.

As her journey progressed, Vanessa discovered the power of connecting with others who had faced similar challenges. She became involved in local support groups and online forums, sharing her experiences and learning from those of others. These connections provided her with valuable insights into coping mechanisms, treatment strategies, and emotional support. By engaging with a community of survivors and caregivers, Vanessa found a sense of solidarity that reinforced her resolve and further fueled her self-advocacy.

Understanding the emotional toll of cancer, Vanessa prioritized her mental health alongside her physical well-being. She sought therapy and participated in wellness programs that focused on mindfulness and stress reduction. Through these practices, she gained a deeper awareness of her own emotional landscape, which in turn allowed her to articulate her needs more effectively to her healthcare team. This holistic approach to her cancer journey underscored the importance of addressing both the physical and psychological aspects of her illness.

Vanessa also became an advocate for health literacy, recognizing that many patients feel overwhelmed and uninformed about their diagnoses. She began to create informational content, blog posts, social media updates, and community workshops. Aimed at demystifying kidney cancer and empowering others to ask questions and seek knowledge. By sharing her own experiences and the lessons she learned along the way, Vanessa hoped to inspire others to take an active role in their health journeys, just as she had.

Her advocacy did not stop at education; Vanessa also became a vocal proponent for access to quality healthcare. She realized that not all patients have the same resources, support systems, or access to information that she had. This awareness spurred her involvement in initiatives aimed at improving healthcare access and equity. Vanessa collaborated with local organizations to raise awareness about the disparities in cancer treatment and worked to ensure that underserved communities received the support and information they needed.

In her advocacy work, Vanessa also focused on promoting the importance of early detection and regular screenings. She understood that raising awareness about kidney cancer could lead to earlier diagnoses, which significantly improve outcomes. Through campaigns and outreach efforts, she encouraged others to prioritize their health, emphasizing that being proactive can make a substantial difference in the fight against cancer.

As Vanessa continued her fight against stage four kidney cancer, she also embraced the role of a mentor. She began to connect with newly diagnosed patients, offering guidance and support based on her own experiences. This mentorship not only provided comfort to others but also reinforced Vanessa's commitment to self-advocacy. By helping others navigate their journeys, she found renewed purpose and strength in her own battle.

The emotional resilience Vanessa developed throughout her journey became a cornerstone of her advocacy. She often shared her story at events, speaking candidly about the highs and lows of living with cancer. Her vulnerability resonated with many, opening up important conversations about the emotional aspects of illness. Vanessa's ability to articulate her struggles and triumphs helped to destigmatize the conversation around cancer, encouraging others to share their own stories and seek support.

In reflecting on her journey, Vanessa recognized that self-advocacy was not a solitary endeavor. It was a collaborative process that involved her medical team, support networks, and the broader community. She learned the value of building relationships with her healthcare providers, emphasizing the importance of trust and open communication. This collaborative approach not only improved her treatment outcomes but also enriched her understanding of what it means to advocate for oneself.

Ultimately, Vanessa's story is one of empowerment and resilience, a beacon of hope for those facing similar challenges. Through her self-advocacy and awareness, she has transformed her battle with stage four kidney cancer into a platform for change. By sharing her journey, educating others, and advocating for equitable healthcare access, Vanessa has not only fought for her own life but has also paved the way for others to reclaim their narratives in the face of adversity. Her legacy is one of courage, knowledge, and compassion, inspiring countless individuals to stand up for their health and well-being.

Vanessa's commitment to self-advocacy extended beyond her personal journey; it evolved into a broader mission to influence change within the healthcare community. She became involved in local advocacy groups focused on kidney cancer awareness, participating in campaigns that aimed to increase funding for research and support services. By sharing her story with lawmakers and community leaders, she drew attention to the urgent need for resources dedicated to kidney cancer, which is often overshadowed by more publicized cancers. Her passion and dedication resonated, and she found herself at the forefront of initiatives that sought to improve patient outcomes and raise awareness about the disease.

Through her advocacy work, Vanessa forged important partnerships with healthcare providers and organizations dedicated to cancer research. She collaborated on educational seminars that educated patients and families about kidney cancer, treatment options, and emerging therapies. These events not only empowered attendees with knowledge but also fostered a sense of community among those affected by the disease. Vanessa's ability to connect with people on personal and emotional levels made her an effective advocate, allowing her to bridge the gap between patients and healthcare professionals.

Moreover, Vanessa recognized the importance of digital platforms in disseminating information and fostering connections. She utilized social media to share her journey, providing real-time updates on her treatment and inviting discussions about coping strategies and triumphs. Her posts garnered a following, inspiring others to engage in conversations about their own experiences with cancer. By cultivating an online community, Vanessa created a safe space for individuals to express their fears, share resources, and support one another through their respective journeys.

As she navigated the complexities of her treatment, Vanessa advocated for more personalized care. She understood that each patient's experience with cancer is unique, and she worked with her medical team to explore treatment options that aligned not just with clinical guidelines but also with her lifestyle and values. This partnership led to a more tailored treatment plan that took into account her preferences and concerns, illustrating the importance of patient-centered care in the oncology field. Vanessa's insistence on individualization underscored the necessity for healthcare providers to listen to and respect their patients' voices.

Vanessa also took on the role of an educator, focusing on the importance of lifestyle factors in cancer management. She began to integrate discussions about nutrition, exercise, and mental wellness into her advocacy efforts. By emphasizing the role that a healthy lifestyle plays in supporting treatment and recovery, she encouraged others to take proactive steps in their own health journeys. Her holistic approach not only addressed the physical aspects of cancer but also highlighted the significance of emotional and mental health, further promoting the idea that well-being is multifaceted.

One of the most impactful aspects of Vanessa's advocacy was her ability to articulate the emotional challenges of living with cancer. She spoke openly about the fear, anxiety, and uncertainty that often accompany a diagnosis, helping to destigmatize these feelings and encouraging others to seek support. By sharing her own vulnerabilities, Vanessa created an atmosphere of authenticity and relatability, allowing those in similar situations to feel seen and understood. Her bravery in discussing these challenges served as a powerful reminder that it's okay to not be okay, fostering a culture of openness among cancer patients.

As Vanessa continues her journey with stage four kidney cancer, her legacy of self-advocacy and awareness remains stronger than ever. She has not only transformed her own experience into a platform for education and support but has also inspired countless others to take charge of their health narratives. Vanessa's story is a shining example of how one individual's courage and determination can lead to meaningful change, both personally and within the broader community. Through her tireless efforts, she has created a ripple effect of empowerment, reminding us all of the importance of standing up for oneself and advocating for equitable healthcare for everyone affected by cancer.

Chapter Thirty One

Learning from Loss

Vanessa's journey through life has been a tapestry woven with vibrant threads of hope and resilience, but when she was diagnosed with stage four kidney cancer, those threads were tested in ways she never imagined. Initially, the news felt like a heavy weight pressing down on her chest, suffocating her with fear and uncertainty. The reality of her diagnosis forced her to confront her mortality, a concept she had only brushed against in philosophical discussions or in the context of others' experiences. As she grappled with this new reality, she began to recognize that her fight against cancer was not just a physical battle, but a profound emotional and spiritual journey.

In the early days of her diagnosis, Vanessa felt an overwhelming sense of isolation. Friends and family offered their support, but the cloud of cancer created a chasm that felt insurmountable. She found solace in journaling, pouring her thoughts onto the pages in a raw and unfiltered manner. Through writing, Vanessa discovered a way to articulate her fears, her hopes, and her experiences. The journal became a confidant, a place where she could explore the depths of her emotions without judgment. This act of self-expression opened a door to healing, allowing her to confront the reality of her condition while also embracing moments of beauty and joy.

As Vanessa underwent treatment, she learned the importance of vulnerability. Each chemotherapy session stripped away another layer of her physical strength, but it also revealed the power of community. She began to open up to those around her, sharing her fears and challenges. This vulnerability fostered deeper connections with her loved ones, who rallied around her in ways she had not anticipated. The outpouring of support illuminated the strength of human connection, teaching her that it was okay to lean on others during times of struggle. Vanessa discovered that in sharing her story, she not only found comfort but also inspired others to confront their own fears and uncertainties.

The diagnosis also prompted Vanessa to reevaluate her priorities. The hectic pace of her previous life, filled with work commitments and social obligations, began to feel trivial in the face of her health crisis. She learned to cherish the small moments. Sipping tea in the morning light, laughing with friends, and feeling the warmth of the sun on her skin. This newfound appreciation for life's simple pleasures became a guiding principle for her. Vanessa realized that often, it is within these small, seemingly insignificant moments that true happiness resides, leading her to a more intentional and fulfilling way of living.

As the months passed, Vanessa developed a profound understanding of the fragility of life. The fear of death, once paralyzing, transformed into a catalyst for change. She began to advocate for herself and others, using her voice to raise awareness about kidney cancer and the importance of early detection. This advocacy became a lifeline, infusing her journey with purpose. Vanessa found strength in her mission, channeling her pain into action that could potentially save lives. This sense of purpose gave her the courage to face the challenges of her illness with grace and determination.

Through the process of treatment, Vanessa also discovered the importance of self-care. The rigorous demands of chemotherapy took a toll on her body, but she learned to listen to her needs. This included not only physical care but also mental and emotional nourishment. She embraced practices such as meditation and mindfulness, which allowed her to find calm amidst the chaos. Vanessa realized that caring for her mind and spirit was just as crucial as caring for her body. This holistic approach to wellness became a cornerstone of her healing journey, providing her with tools to manage stress and anxiety.

In the midst of her struggles, Vanessa also found unexpected moments of joy. She began to notice the beauty in the world around her, from the vibrant colors of the changing seasons to the laughter of children playing in the park. These moments reminded her that life, even in its fragility, holds immense beauty. She cultivated gratitude for each day, recognizing that every sunrise was a gift. This shift in perspective allowed her to approach her illness with a sense of hope and optimism, empowering her to focus on what she could control rather than what she could not.

Vanessa's relationship with her body evolved as well. Initially, she viewed her diagnosis as a betrayal, a body that had once been strong and capable was now failing her. However, as she navigated the complexities of her treatment, she began to see her body in a new light. It became a vessel of resilience, capable of enduring pain and hardship. Vanessa learned to celebrate her body for its strength, for the way it fought tirelessly against the disease. This newfound appreciation transformed her relationship with food, exercise, and self-image, leading her to adopt healthier habits that nourished both her body and soul.

As the reality of living with stage four kidney cancer sunk in, Vanessa also became more attuned to the impermanence of life. She understood that every moment was a fleeting treasure, urging her to live fully in the present. This realization inspired her to seek experiences that would fill her life with meaning and joy. Vanessa made a conscious effort to step outside of her comfort zone, trying new activities that she had always wanted to explore but had previously put off. Whether it was taking a painting class, learning to play the guitar, or going on spontaneous weekend trips, she embraced the philosophy that life is too short to be lived in the shadows of fear. Each new experience became a testament to her resilience, reinforcing the notion that while cancer may have altered her path, it would not define her journey.

Additionally, Vanessa found herself drawn to nature in ways she had never appreciated before. The simple act of walking in the park or hiking in the mountains became a source of healing and rejuvenation. Nature's beauty reminded her of life's cycles, the blooming of flowers, the changing of leaves, and the rhythm of the seasons. She began to incorporate regular outdoor activities into her routine, using these moments to reflect and connect with herself and the world around her. In the embrace of nature, Vanessa discovered a profound sense of peace, allowing her the space to process her feelings and find clarity amidst the chaos of her diagnosis.

As Vanessa continued her battle with cancer, she also began to engage in deeper conversations about life and death with those she loved. These discussions, once regarded as taboo, opened up a new realm of understanding and connection. She realized that sharing her fears and hopes not only alleviated her own anxiety but also encouraged her loved ones to reflect on their own lives. Together, they explored the complexities of existence, the importance of legacy, and the shared human experience of vulnerability. Vanessa found that these conversations were cathartic and enriching, allowing her to forge even stronger bonds with those around her.

Despite the darkness that cancer brought into her life, Vanessa was determined to keep her spirit bright. She started a blog to document her journey, sharing her thoughts, experiences, and the lessons she learned along the way. This platform became a beacon of hope for others facing similar challenges. Through her words, she aimed to inspire courage and resilience in those who felt lost in their struggles. Vanessa's ability to articulate her feelings resonated with many, and as her following grew, she felt a renewed sense of purpose. She was no longer just a patient; she was a voice for others navigating the complexities of illness and healing.

In her blog, Vanessa also explored the concept of gratitude, emphasizing its transformative power. She began a daily practice of writing down three things she was grateful for, no matter how small. This simple act shifted her mindset from one of despair to one of appreciation. Whether it was the warmth of a cup of coffee in the morning or the laughter of a friend, she learned to cherish the moments that brought her joy. This practice became a cornerstone of her emotional resilience, helping her to focus on the positives even in the face of adversity. Gratitude, she discovered, was a powerful antidote to fear and despair.

As Vanessa's journey progressed, she also sought to educate herself about her condition. Knowledge became a source of empowerment as she delved into research about kidney cancer, treatment options, and holistic healing practices. She engaged with her medical team, asking questions and advocating for her own health. This proactive approach not only helped her feel more in control but also instilled a sense of confidence in her treatment decisions. Vanessa learned that understanding her illness was crucial in navigating the complexities of her healthcare, transforming her experience from one of passivity to active engagement.

Through her advocacy and education, Vanessa also became involved in local cancer support groups. Sharing her story and listening to others' experiences provided her with a sense of community that she had longed for. These gatherings became a safe space where individuals could express their fears, hopes, and triumphs without judgment. Vanessa found strength in the shared experiences of others, realizing that they were all on a unique journey yet connected by a common thread of resilience. The support she received from this community became a vital part of her healing process, reinforcing the idea that she was never truly alone in her fight.

Ultimately, Vanessa learned that living with stage four kidney cancer was not solely about battling the disease but about embracing life in all its forms. She recognized that moments of joy could coexist with moments of pain, and that it was possible to find beauty even in the midst of struggle. This duality became her truth, and she vowed to live authentically, honoring both her challenges and her victories. Vanessa understood that her journey would continue to unfold, with its own set of hurdles, but she faced the future with an open heart and a fierce determination to live fully, no matter what lay ahead.

As she reflected on her journey, Vanessa came to a profound realization: life is a series of chapters, each with its own story to tell. She acknowledged the pain of her diagnosis, but she also celebrated the growth it catalyzed. With each passing day, she learned to navigate the complexities.

Chapter Thirty Two

The Power of Gratitude

Vanessa had always been a beacon of positivity, her laughter infectious and her spirit unbreakable. But when she was diagnosed with stage four kidney cancer, her world was turned upside down. It was a moment that would leave many feeling defeated, yet Vanessa found an unexpected source of strength in the power of gratitude. Instead of succumbing to despair, she chose to focus on the blessings in her life, transforming her battle with cancer into a journey of appreciation and resilience.

In the early days of her diagnosis, Vanessa felt overwhelmed by the weight of her circumstances. The prognosis was grim, and the treatment plan daunting. However, rather than allowing fear to consume her, she began to jot down things for which she was grateful. Each morning, she'd write three things that brought her joy, whether it was the warmth of the sun on her face or the laughter of her children echoing through the house. This simple practice became a lifeline, a way to shift her focus from her illness to the beauty surrounding her.

As her treatment progressed, Vanessa faced challenges that tested her resolve. The side effects of chemotherapy were relentless, draining her energy and leaving her feeling vulnerable. Yet, through it all, she continued to embrace gratitude. She often reflected on the compassionate medical team that supported her, the friends who checked in regularly, and the family members who rallied around her. Each gesture of kindness, no matter how small, became a brick in the foundation of her gratitude, fortifying her spirit against the trials of her illness.

Vanessa's perspective on life shifted dramatically during her fight. She began to recognize the importance of savoring each moment. Simple pleasures, like sipping her favorite tea or watching the leaves change colors in the fall, took on new significance. She learned to celebrate the little victories, whether it was a good day in treatment or an evening spent sharing stories with loved ones. Each moment of joy became a testament to her resilience, a reminder that life could still be beautiful even in the face of adversity.

The community that surrounded Vanessa also played a crucial role in her journey. Friends and family organized support groups, creating a network of love and encouragement. Vanessa felt profoundly grateful for their unwavering support, which fueled her determination to fight. These connections reminded her of the power of human connection and the importance of uplifting one another, especially in difficult times. Gratitude became a shared language, fostering a sense of hope and solidarity among those who loved her.

As she navigated the ups and downs of treatment, Vanessa sought to inspire others facing similar battles. She began sharing her story online, emphasizing the power of gratitude in her healing journey. Her posts resonated with many, sparking conversations about the importance of mindset in the face of illness. Through her vulnerability, she encouraged others to find their own sources of gratitude, reminding them that while cancer may change our lives, it does not define us.

Vanessa also discovered that gratitude could manifest in unexpected ways. She learned to appreciate the lessons embedded in her struggle, the resilience she never knew she had, the deeper connections she forged with loved ones, and the newfound clarity about what truly mattered in life. This transformative perspective allowed her to see her cancer journey not solely as a battle but as an opportunity for growth, self-discovery, and deeper appreciation for life's fleeting moments.

Through her journey, Vanessa found joy in giving back. She volunteered with local cancer support organizations, sharing her story and offering encouragement to others. Her gratitude for her own support network inspired her to become a source of hope for those who felt lost or alone. Each time she connected with someone in need, she felt a renewed sense of purpose, reinforcing her belief that gratitude could ripple outwards, creating a wave of positivity and strength within the community.

Despite the ongoing challenges of her diagnosis, Vanessa's spirit remained unyielding. She embraced each day with a heart full of gratitude, understanding that life is a precious gift. Through meditation and mindfulness practices, she cultivated an inner peace that transcended her physical struggles. This inner tranquility became a source of strength, allowing her to face each day with courage and grace. Vanessa's journey was not just about survival; it was about thriving in the midst of adversity.

As time went on, Vanessa often reflected on her journey with gratitude, realizing how far she had come. While the battle with stage four kidney cancer was far from over, she found solace in the knowledge that she was not alone. Her story resonated with many, inspiring others to embrace gratitude as a powerful tool in their own struggles. Vanessa became a symbol of hope, a reminder that even in the darkest moments, there is always something to be grateful for.

In the end, Vanessa's power of gratitude became her greatest weapon against cancer. It shaped her journey, transformed her mindset, and connected her deeply with those around her. She taught others that gratitude is not just a fleeting feeling but a conscious choice. A choice that can illuminate the path ahead, and guide us through our darkest moments. Her unwavering belief in gratitude became a mantra not only for herself but for everyone who encountered her story. Vanessa demonstrated that it is possible to find light amidst the shadows, and that our outlook can significantly impact our experiences. This profound insight became her legacy, transcending her battle with cancer and inspiring countless others to embrace life with open arms, regardless of the circumstances.

As Vanessa continued to share her journey, she began organizing gratitude alliances within her community. These gatherings became safe spaces for individuals facing hardships to come together and practice gratitude. Participants shared their own stories, creating a tapestry of resilience woven from their collective experiences. Vanessa facilitated discussions on the power of gratitude, encouraging attendees to reflect on their own lives and find moments of appreciation, even when faced with difficulties. The alliances fostered a sense of camaraderie as shared experiences created bonds that transcended mere acquaintanceship.

During one alliance, a young woman approached Vanessa, tears in her eyes. She shared how she had been struggling with her own health issues and felt isolated in her pain. Vanessa listened intently, her heart swelling with empathy. With gentle encouragement, she prompted the woman to identify small things in her life that brought her joy. Together, they crafted a gratitude list. A simple yet powerful tool that sparked a shift in the woman's perspective. As she began to recognize the beauty in her life, the heaviness of her struggles seemed to lighten. Vanessa realized that her own journey had the potential to create ripples of change in the lives of others.

In the midst of her workshops, Vanessa also found time to connect with fellow cancer patients. She joined online support groups, not only to seek help but to offer it. Sharing her story of gratitude in these settings resonated deeply with others who felt overwhelmed by their diagnoses. She listened to their fears, their hopes, and their struggles, gently reminding them of the importance of finding light in the darkness. Vanessa's authenticity and warmth created a safe space for vulnerability, allowing others to open up and begin their own journeys of gratitude and healing.

As the months passed and her health fluctuated, Vanessa remained committed to her gratitude practice. She continued to write in her journal, documenting the moments of joy and connection that filled her days. On particularly challenging days, when fatigue threatened to overwhelm her, she would revisit her earlier entries, reminding herself of the beauty she had witnessed. This ritual served as a powerful reminder that while her body may be weakened, her spirit remained strong. It reinforced her belief that gratitude could coexist with pain and uncertainty.

Vanessa's story began to attract attention beyond her immediate community. Friends featured her journey, highlighting her unique approach to coping with cancer. She became a symbol of hope, and her message of gratitude resonated with many. People from all walks of life reached out to her, sharing their own stories and expressing how her perspective had impacted their lives. With each message of support, Vanessa felt her mission to spread gratitude growing stronger. She understood that her journey could inspire others to find their strength, no matter the challenges they faced.

In the face of ongoing treatment, Vanessa's health would occasionally take a downturn, but she approached each setback with resilience. She learned to allow herself to feel the pain, to acknowledge the hardships, while simultaneously seeking out the silver linings. The support of her family and friends became even more crucial during these times, as they rallied around her, reminding her of the strength she had cultivated. It was a beautiful symbiotic relationship. Her gratitude fueled their support, and their love fueled her gratitude.

As the seasons changed, Vanessa found herself reflecting on her journey more deeply. She began to see her battle with cancer as part of a larger narrative. A story of growth, connection, and transformation. Each experience she had faced, each person she had met, contributed to a profound understanding of life's fragility and its beauty. She realized that her journey was not solely about overcoming illness but about embracing the fullness of life in all its complexities. This understanding deepened her gratitude, and she felt a renewed sense of purpose.

Vanessa's commitment to gratitude also extended to her family, encouraging them to adopt similar practices. They began hosting family gratitude nights, where each member shared what they were thankful for that week. These gatherings became cherished traditions, fostering deeper connections and reminding them all of the love that surrounded them. Vanessa marveled at how a simple act of sharing gratitude could strengthen their bonds and create a sense of unity, even in the face of uncertainty.

Eventually, as Vanessa's journey continued, she began to dream of turning her writing journal into a book to share her experiences. She envisioned a collection of stories, reflections, and practical exercises that would guide others in harnessing the power of gratitude. Her hope was that it would serve as a companion for those navigating their own challenges, offering them the tools to find light even in the darkest times. This vision became a new goal, one that fueled her determination.

Chapter Thirty Three

Facing Recurrence: A New Challenge

After months of fighting stage four kidney cancer with a sense of gratitude that had transformed her outlook on life, Vanessa faced a new challenge that would test her resilience once again. During a routine check-up, her oncologist delivered the news that no one ever wants to hear. The cancer had returned, this time with a vengeance. The initial shock resonated through her body, and for a moment, she felt as though the ground had shifted beneath her feet. However, Vanessa quickly reminded herself of her journey. A journey defined by strength, hope, and the power of gratitude.

In the days following the diagnosis, Vanessa found herself grappling with a whirlwind of emotions. Doubts crept in, and fear whispered insidiously in her ear. Yet, amidst the uncertainty, she made a conscious decision to confront this new challenge head-on. Drawing upon her previous experiences, she began to create a plan. One that involved not only her medical treatment but also a renewed commitment to gratitude. She returned to her journal, documenting her feelings, fears, and hopes. Journaling became her refuge, a way to channel her emotions into something constructive.

As Vanessa embarked on her new treatment regimen, she chose to approach each day with intention. She began her mornings with meditation, focusing on the things she was grateful for. Her supportive family, the beauty of the world around her, and the moments of joy that still punctuated her life. This practice grounded her, providing a sense of clarity amid the chaos. She understood that while the road ahead would be challenging, maintaining a grateful heart would be essential in navigating the storm.

Vanessa also reached out to her network of fellow cancer warriors. Those who had walked similar paths and had emerged with wisdom to share. Connecting with them became a source of inspiration. They exchanged stories of resilience, strategies for coping with setbacks, and words of encouragement that fueled her spirit. In these conversations, Vanessa found solace; she was not alone in this fight. Each shared experience reinforced her belief that community and connection are powerful allies in the face of adversity.

Amidst her treatment, Vanessa made a conscious effort to engage in activities that brought her joy. She resumed her gratitude alliances, using them as a platform to share her journey with others. The alliances took on a new dimension, as she spoke openly about the recurrence of her cancer and how gratitude had been her anchor throughout the process. Participants resonated with her vulnerability, and many expressed that her willingness to share both her struggles and triumphs empowered them to embrace their own challenges.

In her personal life, Vanessa leaned heavily on her family for support. They became her cheerleaders, celebrating small victories and offering comfort during difficult days. It was during one of these intimate moments that her daughter presented her with a handmade gratitude jar. Each family member contributed notes of appreciation, filling the jar with reminders of love and support. This simple act became a cherished ritual, reinforcing their bond and serving as a tangible reminder of the light that existed even in the darkest times.

As the weeks turned into months, Vanessa faced the physical toll of her treatment. The fatigue was overwhelming, and there were days when the weight of her diagnosis felt insurmountable. However, she learned to listen to her body and rest when needed. On particularly tough days, she would revisit her gratitude journal, allowing the power of her words to uplift her spirit. Each entry served as a reminder of her strength and the beauty that still existed in her life, pushing her to persevere.

One pivotal moment in her journey came during a family outing to a local park. Surrounded by nature, laughter, and the warmth of her loved ones, Vanessa felt a profound sense of peace wash over her. In that moment of clarity, she realized that while cancer was a formidable opponent, it did not define her. The love, joy, and gratitude she cultivated were far more powerful than any diagnosis. This epiphany ignited a fire within her, fueling her determination to continue fighting with everything she had.

Vanessa's unwavering spirit began to inspire others around her, not just those battling cancer but anyone facing their own challenges. She created an online platform where she shared her journey, focusing on the importance of gratitude and resilience. Her message resonated widely, and she began receiving messages from strangers who found hope in her story. Each connection reinforced her belief that vulnerability could be a source of strength, and that sharing her journey could light the way for others.

As Vanessa approached the end of her treatment cycle, she felt a renewed sense of hope. While the uncertainty of her future remained, she had cultivated a mindset that allowed her to embrace each day with gratitude. She understood that life was unpredictable, but her journey had taught her the importance of cherishing the present moment. With her family by her side, she celebrated the milestones, both big and small, finding joy in the simple act of being alive.

Ultimately, Vanessa emerged from this new challenge not just as a cancer survivor but as a beacon of hope and resilience. She realized that her journey through stage four kidney cancer had transformed her in ways she had never anticipated. The recurrence of her illness had deepened her understanding of gratitude, teaching her that it is not merely a reaction to good fortune but a choice, a commitment to finding beauty even in the face of adversity. This transformative experience became a cornerstone of her identity, one that she was eager to share with the world.

With her health stabilizing, Vanessa decided to further amplify her message by collaborating with local hospitals and cancer support organizations. She organized gatherings centered around gratitude, inviting healthcare professionals, patients, and their families to participate in gatherings that focused on mindfulness and appreciation. These gatherings became a celebration of life, where laughter mingled with tears, and stories of hope were shared freely. Vanessa's ability to connect with people from all walks of life helped foster a community that thrived on support and understanding.

One particularly memorable event was held in honor of Cancer Awareness Month. Vanessa invited a panel of survivors to share their journeys, highlighting not only the challenges they faced but also the lessons they learned along the way. She moderated the discussion, weaving in her own experiences with humor and vulnerability. The room was filled with emotions as participants resonated with stories of triumph, grief, and everything in between. The event left a lasting impact on attendees, reinforcing the idea that gratitude could coexist with pain and that there was strength in vulnerability.

Encouraged by the positive response, Vanessa took a leap of faith and began drafting her journal. A culmination of her experiences, reflections, and practical exercises designed to help others embrace gratitude in their own lives. She poured her heart into her writing process, weaving together anecdotes and lessons learned from her journey. As she wrote, she felt a sense of liberation; her story was no longer just her own; it was a gift to anyone struggling with their own challenges.

As she neared the completion of her journal, Vanessa reached out to other authors, seeking guidance on the publishing process. She was met with kindness and support, which fueled her determination to see the project through. The act of sharing her story became a cathartic experience, allowing her to process her feelings and solidify her understanding of the power of gratitude. Each word written was a step toward healing, both for herself and for those who would read her story.

Vanessa's journey was not without its struggles, however. There were days when self-doubt crept in, and she questioned whether her story was worthy of being shared. Yet, with the encouragement of her family and friends, she pushed through the insecurities. Her mantra became a reminder. "Your story matters." This realization reignited her passion and propelled her forward, reminding her that vulnerability can be a source of strength that inspires others to embrace their own narratives.

As her journal neared publication, Vanessa also began to explore ways to expand her impact beyond her local community. She launched an article where she could engage in conversations with other cancer survivors, mental health advocates, and wellness experts. Each episode was infused with heartfelt stories, practical advice, and discussions on the importance of gratitude and resilience. The article quickly gained traction, creating a platform for connection and support that resonated with listeners.

With the release of her journal and the growing success of her article, Vanessa felt an overwhelming sense of fulfillment. She had turned her pain into purpose, and in doing so, she had created a legacy that extended beyond her own experiences. The messages she received from readers and listeners who found comfort and hope in her words confirmed that she was making a difference. In sharing her journey, she had illuminated a path for others, encouraging them to find their own strength and embrace life's challenges with gratitude.

As Vanessa continued to navigate her own health journey, she remained steadfast in her commitment to living in the moment. She understood that life was unpredictable, but she had learned the importance of celebrating each day and cherishing the connections she had fostered. With her family by her side, she embraced the beauty of life, knowing that every moment was a gift worth appreciating. Through her resilience, vulnerability, and unwavering spirit, Vanessa had transformed her battle with stage four kidney cancer into a story of hope, inspiring countless others to find their own light in the darkness.

Chapter Thirty Four

The Role of Nutrition and Wellness

As Vanessa faced the daunting challenge of stage four kidney cancer, she quickly recognized that nutrition and wellness would play a crucial role in her overall treatment plan. Initially overwhelmed by the diagnosis, she sought information on how dietary choices could influence her health, energy levels, and quality of life during this difficult journey. Understanding that her body was under immense stress, Vanessa was determined to equip herself with the tools necessary to support her physical and emotional well-being.

Vanessa began her journey by consulting with a registered dietitian who specialized in oncology nutrition. Together, they created a personalized meal plan designed to nourish her body while considering the unique challenges posed by her cancer. The dietitian emphasized the importance of maintaining a balanced intake of proteins, healthy fats, and carbohydrates, all while ensuring that Vanessa was getting the vitamins and minerals essential for her immune system. This collaboration empowered Vanessa with knowledge and practical strategies to make informed choices about her diet.

One of the significant changes Vanessa implemented was increasing her intake of fruits and vegetables. Rich in antioxidants, vitamins, and fiber, these foods became staples in her diet. She discovered the importance of colorful foods, which not only provided essential nutrients but also made her meals visually appealing. Vanessa found joy in experimenting with new recipes and flavors, transforming her kitchen into a space of creativity and healing. This new culinary adventure became a source of solace, allowing her to focus on nourishing her body rather than the disease that threatened it.

Hydration also emerged as a key component of Vanessa's wellness strategy. She learned that staying well-hydrated was essential for her kidneys, especially while undergoing treatment. Vanessa made a conscious effort to drink plenty of water throughout the day, incorporating herbal teas and infused water with fresh fruits and herbs to keep things interesting. She found that hydration not only helped her physically but also boosted her mood, allowing her to feel more energized and alert.

In addition to nutrition, Vanessa recognized the importance of integrating wellness practices into her daily routine. She explored various forms of exercise that suited her energy levels, focusing on gentle activities such as yoga and walking. These practices not only helped her maintain physical strength but also provided a sense of calm and grounding. Vanessa embraced the idea that movement could be a form of meditation, allowing her to connect with her body and foster a sense of peace amid the turmoil of her diagnosis.

Mindfulness and stress management became essential components of her wellness journey. Vanessa began practicing meditation and deep breathing exercises to help manage anxiety and promote relaxation. She attended guided meditation sessions and explored mindfulness apps that offered support during difficult moments. These practices taught her to be present and find gratitude in the small things, even on the days when her energy waned. The combination of nutritious food and mindfulness helped create a holistic approach to her healing.

Vanessa also sought support from holistic wellness practitioners who offered additional modalities, such as acupuncture and herbal medicine. These therapies complemented her conventional treatment and provided her with tools to manage side effects and improve her overall well-being. The acupuncture sessions helped alleviate pain and discomfort, while herbal supplements were carefully chosen to support her immune function. Vanessa learned the importance of communicating openly with her medical team about these therapies to ensure they were part of a cohesive plan.

As she navigated her wellness journey, Vanessa became increasingly aware of the emotional and mental aspects of cancer treatment. She engaged in support groups where she connected with others facing similar challenges. Sharing her experiences and learning from others became a crucial source of encouragement and strength. Vanessa realized that nutrition and wellness extended beyond physical health; they encompassed emotional resilience and community support, both vital in the fight against cancer.

Through her commitment to nutrition and wellness, Vanessa also discovered the power of self-advocacy. She learned to listen to her body and respond to its needs, whether that meant adjusting her diet based on how she felt or advocating for complementary therapies alongside her medical treatments. This newfound sense of agency empowered her to take charge of her health, reinforcing the idea that she was not merely a passive recipient of treatment but an active participant in her healing journey.

As Vanessa continued to embrace nutrition and wellness, she began to notice positive changes in her overall well-being. Her energy levels improved, and she felt more in control of her body and mind. Friends and family remarked on her vibrant spirit and determination, which only fueled her passion for sharing her journey with others. Vanessa became an advocate for the importance of nutrition and holistic wellness in cancer care, believing that every patient deserves to feel empowered and supported.

Ultimately, Vanessa's commitment to nutrition and wellness became not only a personal journey but a message of hope for others facing similar battles. She began sharing her story through workshops and social media, emphasizing the transformative power of making mindful choices. By highlighting the role of nutrition in cancer recovery, Vanessa inspired others to explore how they could take charge of their health and well-being, fostering a sense of community and resilience among cancer warriors everywhere.

As Vanessa continued to share her journey and insights on nutrition and wellness, she felt a profound sense of purpose and connection with her audience. She focused on educating others about the significance of dietary choices during cancer treatment. Her audience became safe spaces for sharing stories, exchanging tips, and fostering support among attendees. The energy in the room was palpable as participants engaged in discussions about their experiences, and Vanessa found joy in facilitating these meaningful conversations.

During these conversations Vanessa emphasized the importance of personalized nutrition. She often shared her own journey of working with a registered dietitian, encouraging others to seek professional guidance tailored to their specific needs. Vanessa spoke candidly about how certain foods made her feel, illustrating the profound connection between diet and emotional well-being. She illustrated her points with visual aids, showcasing colorful plates filled with fresh produce and whole grains, demonstrating that healthy eating could be both nourishing and delightful.

One of the highlights of her self advocacy was the cooking demonstrations. Vanessa created healthy dishes that were both flavorful and easy to prepare. Family and friends eagerly participated, chopping vegetables, mixing ingredients, and tasting the final products. These interactive sessions not only equipped family and friends with practical skills but also fostered a sense of friendship and love, as they bonded over their shared commitment to improving their health. Vanessa reveled in the joy of cooking together, knowing that these moments were pivotal in building support.

As her audience gained popularity, Vanessa expanded her outreach to further online platforms. She launched articles dedicated to nutrition and wellness during cancer treatment, offering resources, recipes, and articles that highlighted the importance of mindful eating. Vanessa utilized social media to share bite-sized tips, infographics, and personal reflections, reaching a wider audience beyond her local community. She was thrilled to receive messages from individuals around the world who found inspiration in her story and were eager to implement healthier habits in their own lives.

Recognizing the power of storytelling, Vanessa invited guests to share their own experiences on her platform. She sought interviews with nutritionists, survivors, and wellness practitioners, creating a rich tapestry of voices that resonated with her audience. Each story added depth to her message, illustrating the diverse paths people take in their healing journeys. Vanessa understood that everyone's experience with cancer is unique, and by sharing various perspectives, she could foster a sense of belonging and understanding among her followers.

Vanessa also began writing articles for wellness and cancer support blogs, further amplifying her voice in the conversation about nutrition and cancer care. Her writings emphasized the importance of finding joy in food, encouraging individuals to view cooking and eating as acts of self-care rather than chores. She shared tips on how to cultivate a positive relationship with food, highlighting the idea that nourishment goes beyond mere calories; it encompasses comfort, connection, and celebration of life.

In her self advocacy, Vanessa remained acutely aware of the challenges many individuals faced during cancer treatment. She often addressed issues such as nausea, loss of appetite, and dietary restrictions, offering practical solutions and alternatives based on her own experiences. She collaborated with healthcare professionals to create resources that would help patients navigate these obstacles with confidence. Vanessa's compassionate approach resonated deeply with those who felt overwhelmed, offering them hope and practical strategies to improve their quality of life.

Each opportunity allowed her to connect with other advocates, researchers, and healthcare providers who were equally passionate about improving patient outcomes. Vanessa felt honored to be part of a larger movement advocating for holistic approaches to cancer treatment, emphasizing the integration of nutrition and wellness into conventional care.

Through her journey, Vanessa also learned the importance of self-care beyond nutrition. She began to prioritize activities that brought her joy, whether it was painting, gardening, or spending time with loved ones. Understanding that mental and emotional health are intertwined with physical health, she encouraged her audience to make time for self-care practices that nourish their souls. This holistic view of wellness became a central theme in her message, reminding others that healing is a multifaceted journey.

Ultimately, Vanessa's commitment to nutrition and wellness evolved into a mission to empower others facing cancer. She became a guiding light for those navigating similar paths, reminding them that they have the power to influence their health through mindful choices. By sharing her knowledge, experiences, and passion for healthy living, Vanessa created a community of support and inspiration that extended far beyond her own journey, leaving a lasting impact on the lives of many. She had transformed her battle with stage four kidney cancer into a movement of hope, resilience, and the belief that wellness is possible, even in the face of adversity.

Chapter Thirty Five

Mindfulness, Rest, and Meditation

Mindfulness, rest, and meditation can be powerful tools in the journey of battling stage four kidney cancer. The diagnosis itself can feel overwhelming, bringing a barrage of emotions that may include fear, sadness, and uncertainty. Amidst these tumultuous feelings, the practice of mindfulness offers a grounding force, allowing individuals to focus on the present moment rather than becoming consumed by the weight of what lies ahead. By cultivating an awareness of the here and now, patients can begin to reclaim a sense of control over their thoughts and emotions, creating a buffer against the anxiety often associated with cancer treatment.

Rest is equally crucial in this journey. The body undergoes immense stress during cancer treatment, and adequate rest is essential for physical recovery and emotional well-being. Sleep disturbances are common in cancer patients, exacerbating feelings of fatigue and anxiety. By prioritizing rest, individuals can enhance their resilience and improve their overall quality of life. Establishing a soothing bedtime routine, which may include mindfulness practices or meditation, can pave the way for deeper, more restorative sleep, allowing the body to heal and rejuvenate.

Meditation serves as a bridge between mindfulness and rest. It provides a structured approach to cultivating awareness and promoting relaxation. For cancer patients, meditation can be a sanctuary. A space to retreat from the chaos of treatment, doctor appointments, and medical jargon. Guided meditation, in particular, can be especially beneficial, allowing individuals to connect with their breath and body while being gently led through visualizations that promote healing and peace. This practice not only helps to quiet the mind but also aids in reducing physical discomfort and emotional turmoil.

The integration of mindfulness into daily routines can create a significant shift in perspective for those facing cancer. Simple practices, such as mindful eating or walking, can transform ordinary moments into opportunities for connection and gratitude. In the midst of treatment, patients may find solace in appreciating the small joys, a warm cup of tea, the laughter of loved ones, or the beauty of nature. These moments of mindfulness can serve as anchors, reminding individuals that life continues amidst the challenges of illness.

Mindfulness, rest, and meditation also foster a supportive environment for emotional expression. Cancer can bring about a complex array of feelings, and often, patients may struggle to articulate their experiences. Mindfulness encourages individuals to acknowledge their emotions without judgment. By creating space for feelings of fear, anger, or sadness, patients can process their experiences more fully, finding a sense of relief in the acknowledgment of their journey. This emotional release can be empowering, allowing patients to reclaim their narrative and approach their treatment with renewed strength.

Incorporating these practices into a daily routine can also enhance the effectiveness of medical treatments. Studies have shown that mindfulness and meditation can reduce stress and anxiety, leading to improvements in immune function and overall health. For cancer patients, this means that engaging in mindfulness practices could potentially complement their medical regimen, fostering a more holistic approach to healing. As patients learn to manage their stress and cultivate a positive mindset, they may find that they are better equipped to handle the challenges that arise during treatment.

Support from loved ones can amplify the benefits of mindfulness and meditation. Sharing the practice with family and friends can foster a sense of community and belonging, which is especially vital during a cancer diagnosis.

Group meditation sessions, for example, can create a collective space for healing, where participants can share their experiences and support one another. This connection not only enhances the emotional benefits of mindfulness but also reinforces the importance of social support in navigating the cancer journey.

As patients progress through their treatment, the practice of mindfulness can evolve. What begins as a tool for managing anxiety may develop into a deeper exploration of self-awareness and acceptance. Patients may find that mindfulness helps them cultivate resilience, enabling them to face the ups and downs of their journey with grace. This evolving relationship with mindfulness can empower individuals to redefine their experience of cancer, shifting from a narrative of fear to one of strength and possibility.

Additionally, the practice of mindfulness can inspire patients to advocate for their own well-being. By fostering a deeper understanding of their thoughts and feelings, individuals may feel more empowered to communicate openly with their healthcare team. This increased awareness can lead to more informed decision-making and a greater sense of agency in their treatment journey. Patients who embrace mindfulness may find themselves more attuned to their bodies, better able to recognize when something feels off, and more confident in voicing their concerns.

In a world that often emphasizes the urgency of treatment and results, mindfulness reminds patients to slow down and honor their own experience. Each day presents an opportunity to practice acceptance, to embrace the complexities of cancer, and to find peace in the midst of turmoil. Ultimately, the journey through stage four kidney cancer is deeply personal, and the integration of mindfulness, rest, and meditation can illuminate a path towards healing. A journey marked not only by the challenges of illness but also by moments of profound beauty, connection, and resilience.

In conclusion, mindfulness, rest, and meditation are invaluable allies for those navigating the challenges of stage four kidney cancer. These practices offer a means to cultivate inner peace and resilience, fostering a sense of agency in a situation that can often feel disempowering. By focusing on the present moment, patients can learn to manage their stress and anxiety, allowing them to approach their treatment with a clearer mind and a more open heart. Emphasizing the importance of self-care, these practices remind individuals that their emotional and mental well-being is just as crucial as their physical health in the fight against cancer.

Moreover, the journey through cancer is often marked by uncertainty and unpredictability. Mindfulness teaches patients to embrace this uncertainty rather than resist it. By developing an attitude of acceptance, individuals can find freedom in letting go of the need to control every outcome. This shift in mindset can be liberating, allowing patients to engage more fully with their lives, regardless of their diagnosis. Instead of being defined solely by their illness, they can cultivate a broader sense of identity that includes their interests, passions, and relationships.

Rest plays a pivotal role in this transformative journey. The physical toll of cancer and its treatment can lead to profound fatigue, making restorative sleep essential. Patients who prioritize rest,and create an environment that supports it, can enhance their overall well-being. This may involve establishing a calming nighttime ritual, such as gentle stretching or reading, which can pave the way for a more restful night. As the body receives the rest it needs, patients may find themselves better equipped to face the challenges of treatment, both physically and emotionally.

Additionally, the practice of meditation can serve as a form of self-compassion. Through guided meditations focused on healing and self-love, patients can cultivate a nurturing relationship with themselves. In a world that often emphasizes productivity and achievement, patients may feel guilty for taking time to rest or meditate. However, these practices reinforce the notion that self-care is not only a necessity but a fundamental aspect of healing. By acknowledging their own needs and prioritizing their well-being, individuals can foster a deeper sense of compassion for themselves, making space for healing and growth.

As cancer patients connect with mindfulness, rest, and meditation, they may also discover the power of gratitude. This transformative practice allows individuals to shift their focus from what is lacking or difficult to what is present and supportive. By recognizing and appreciating even the smallest blessings, be it a supportive friend, a moment of peace, or a beautiful sunset. Patients can cultivate a positive outlook that nurtures their spirit. This practice can be particularly impactful during treatment, as it helps individuals find joy amidst the challenges, creating a buffer against despair.

Moreover, sharing these practices with others can create a ripple effect of healing. Whether through support groups, family gatherings, or community workshops, patients can invite their loved ones into their journey of mindfulness and meditation. This shared experience not only fosters connection but also helps to normalize discussions of mental and emotional health in the context of cancer. As loved ones become more aware of the importance of self-care, they may also adopt these practices in their own lives, creating a culture of support and understanding that extends beyond the illness.

Ultimately, the integration of mindfulness, rest, and meditation into the lives of those facing stage four kidney cancer can lead to a profound transformation. These practices empower individuals to take an active role in their healing journey, emphasizing the interconnectedness of mind, body, and spirit. By fostering resilience, acceptance, and gratitude, patients can navigate the complexities of cancer with greater ease and grace. The journey may be fraught with challenges, but through mindfulness and self-compassion, individuals can discover a deeper sense of purpose and meaning, transforming their relationship with illness and illuminating a path toward healing.

Chapter Thirty Six

Reflections on Resilience

Vanessa's journey with stage four kidney cancer began as a bewildering and terrifying experience. She vividly recalls the day she received her diagnosis, a moment etched in her memory. The words "stage four" echoed in her mind like a haunting refrain, filling her with an overwhelming sense of dread. Initially, she felt like she had been thrust into a dark tunnel with no clear way out. But as the shock began to wane, Vanessa realized that this was not just a battle against the disease; it was a profound test of her resilience and spirit.

As the weeks turned into months, Vanessa discovered a strength within herself that she never knew existed. Each Radvax therapy session was not just a medical procedure; it became a ritual of empowerment. She transformed the sterile hospital room into her own sacred space, surrounding herself with photographs, notes from friends, and her favorite music. This environment helped her redefine what it meant to be a patient. Instead of feeling like a victim, she embraced the role of a warrior, determined to fight back against the cancer that threatened her life.

Support from family and friends played a pivotal role in her resilience. Vanessa recalls the countless phone calls, messages, and visits from loved ones who rallied around her during her darkest moments. These connections became lifelines, reminding her that she was not alone in this fight. She learned the importance of vulnerability, allowing herself to lean on others when the weight of her illness felt unbearable. Each shared laugh, tear, and moment of silence with those she loved reinforced her belief that community is a powerful source of strength.

In the midst of her treatment, Vanessa began to explore the concept of gratitude. She started a journal where she would write down three things she was grateful for each day. It was a simple practice, but it changed her perspective. She found joy in the small things, a sunny day, a delicious meal, or a heartfelt conversation. This shift towards gratitude didn't erase the pain or fear of her illness, but it added a layer of lightness and hope to her journey. It became a reminder that even in suffering, there were moments worth cherishing.

Vanessa's resilience was also shaped by her desire to advocate for others facing similar battles. She began attending support groups, sharing her story, and listening to others. This exchange of experiences fostered a sense of camaraderie that was both healing and empowering. Vanessa realized that her journey could serve as inspiration for others, and she found purpose in helping them navigate their own challenges. This newfound mission gave her a reason to wake up each day with intention and hope.

Throughout her treatment, Vanessa encountered many setbacks, including unexpected complications and moments of intense fear. Yet, each time she faced adversity, she dug deep within herself to find courage. She learned to reframe her thoughts, focusing on what she could control rather than what was beyond her reach. This mental shift became a crucial tool in her resilience toolkit, helping her to confront the reality of her illness with a sense of agency and determination.

Art became another outlet for Vanessa's resilience. She began painting as a form of therapy, allowing her emotions to flow onto the canvas. Each brushstroke was a release, a way to express the tumult of feelings she experienced during her battle with cancer. The process was cathartic, and the colors she chose reflected her journey, from dark shades of fear to vibrant hues of hope. Through art, Vanessa found a voice for her struggles and triumphs, creating a visual narrative of her resilience.

As months went by, Vanessa realized that resilience wasn't just about fighting cancer; it was about embracing life in its entirety. She made a conscious effort to celebrate her milestones, no matter how small. Whether it was completing a round of treatment or simply enjoying a day without pain, these moments became markers of her journey. Vanessa learned to recognize the power of each day, savoring experiences that reminded her of what truly mattered in life, love, connection, and the beauty of being present.

The experience of battling stage four kidney cancer ultimately transformed Vanessa's view of herself and her world. She emerged from her journey with a newfound appreciation for life's fragility and the strength that resides within. Resilience, she realized, was not a destination but a continuous process of growth and adaptation. Each challenge she faced added depth to her character, teaching her lessons in compassion, patience, and perseverance.

Today, Vanessa is an advocate for cancer awareness, sharing her story to inspire others. Driven by a desire to make a difference in the lives of those affected by cancer. Her reflections on resilience have become a beacon of hope for many, reminding them that even in the face of insurmountable odds, the human spirit has an incredible capacity to endure and thrive.

In her quiet moments, Vanessa often reflects on her journey, grateful for the lessons learned and the relationships forged along the way. She understands that while cancer may have changed her, it did not define her. Instead, it became a chapter in her life story. A narrative of resilience, courage, and transformation. Each day, Vanessa wakes up with a renewed sense of purpose, committed to living fully and authentically. The fear of recurrence lingers in the background, but she refuses to let it dictate her life. Instead, she channels that energy into positivity, focusing on the present and all the possibilities it holds.

Vanessa has also developed a deeper understanding of the importance of self-care. Initially, she viewed self-care as a luxury, something to be indulged in once her cancer battle was over. However, through her experience, she learned that self-care is essential for sustaining resilience. Whether it's practicing mindfulness, engaging in physical activity, or simply taking a long, soothing bath, these moments of self-nurturing have become integral to her daily routine. They serve as reminders that caring for oneself is not selfish but necessary for maintaining strength in the face of adversity.

Her journey has also sparked a profound interest in holistic wellness. Vanessa began exploring alternative therapies, such as yoga and meditation, which complemented her conventional treatment. These practices helped her cultivate a sense of inner peace and centeredness, allowing her to navigate the emotional turbulence of her illness. She found solace in the gentle movements of yoga and the calming effects of meditation, integrating them into her life as tools for resilience and healing.

Sharing her story has become a vital part of Vanessa's healing process. She has taken to social media to connect with others who are going through similar struggles. Her posts resonate with many, as she candidly shares her experiences, including the raw and vulnerable moments that accompany a cancer diagnosis. The response has been overwhelmingly positive, with messages from individuals who feel inspired by her strength and authenticity. This virtual community has not only provided support for others but has also reinforced her own sense of connection and purpose.

Vanessa's advocacy extends beyond sharing her story; she actively participates in community outreach programs that promote cancer awareness and education. She believes that knowledge is power, and by educating others about the signs and symptoms of kidney cancer, she can help facilitate early detection, which is crucial for better outcomes. She often collaborates with local organizations to host workshops and events, creating spaces for open dialogue about cancer and its impact on individuals and families. Through these initiatives, she feels a sense of fulfillment, knowing she is contributing to a cause greater than herself.

As Vanessa continues to navigate her life post-treatment, she has also embraced the concept of living with intention. She has set new goals for herself, both personally and professionally. Whether it's traveling to places she has always dreamed of visiting, pursuing hobbies she had set aside, or even considering further education, she has adopted a mindset that encourages her to seize opportunities without hesitation. Each goal accomplished is a testament to her resilience. A reminder that life is not just about survival but about thriving.

The friendships she has built with fellow cancer survivors have become a cherished aspect of her life. These relationships are characterized by an unspoken understanding, a bond forged through shared struggles and triumphs. They provide a safe space for each other to express fears and hopes, creating a unique camaraderie that transcends the challenges of cancer. Vanessa often reflects on the importance of these connections, recognizing that they enrich her journey and remind her that she is part of a larger community of survivors.

Ultimately, Vanessa's reflections on resilience and her battle with stage four kidney cancer have shaped her into a person who embraces life with open arms. She understands that resilience is not merely about enduring hardship but about finding joy in the journey, regardless of its challenges. Through her experiences, she has learned to appreciate the beauty of vulnerability and the strength that comes from it. As she looks to the future, Vanessa carries with her the lessons of her past, determined to live a life that honors her journey and inspires others to do the same.

Chapter Thirty Seven

The Healing Power of Love

Vanessa's experience with Radvax therapy in her fight against cancer was transformative, not only in terms of her physical health but also in the profound healing power of love that surrounded her during this journey. From the moment she began her treatment, she felt a palpable sense of support from her family, friends, and healthcare team. This love created a nurturing environment that played a crucial role in her healing process. It was as if each dose of Radvax was infused with the collective energy and compassion of those who cared for her, offering her hope and strength in every moment of uncertainty.

One of the most significant aspects of her healing journey was the unwavering support from her family. They rallied around her, creating a sanctuary of love and encouragement. Vanessa recalls the countless nights spent with her loved ones, sharing stories and laughter that helped ease her anxiety. Their presence provided her with a sense of belonging and reassurance, reminding her that she was never alone in this fight. The warmth of their love acted as a balm, soothing her fears and instilling in her a belief that healing was possible.

Her friends, too, became a vital source of love and support. They organized a series of "healing circles," where they gathered to meditate, pray, and send positive energy her way. These gatherings became a sacred space for Vanessa, where she could feel the collective intention and love of those around her. Each gathering reinforced her belief in the power of community and connection, reminding her that love could transcend even the most challenging circumstances. It was during these moments that she truly understood how love could amplify her resilience, acting as a powerful force against the pain and uncertainty of her diagnosis.

The healthcare professionals involved in her Radvax therapy also played a crucial role in her experience of love and healing. Vanessa felt a genuine care from her doctors and nurses, who not only treated her body but also acknowledged her emotional and spiritual well-being. Their compassionate approach made her feel seen and valued as a person, not just as a patient. This connection fostered a sense of trust, allowing her to engage more fully in her treatment. Each interaction was infused with kindness, reinforcing her belief that love was an essential component of her healing journey.

As Vanessa progressed through her Radvax therapy, she began to realize that love also came in unexpected forms. She found solace in the kindness of strangers, whether it was a fellow patient sharing a smile or a nurse offering words of encouragement during a tough day. These small acts of kindness added up, creating a tapestry of love that enveloped her in moments when she needed it most. It became clear to her that love could be found everywhere, and these connections, however brief, contributed significantly to her sense of hope and healing.

Vanessa also discovered the importance of self-love during her treatment. Initially, she grappled with feelings of guilt and frustration over her illness, questioning her worth and purpose. However, through reflection and support, she learned the significance of being compassionate towards herself. Practicing self-love involved acknowledging her feelings, celebrating her small victories, and allowing herself to rest when needed. This shift in perspective was empowering, as it fostered a deeper connection with her own spirit. Reminding her that she was deserving of love, both from others and from within.

Throughout her treatment, Vanessa became increasingly aware of the healing power of love in the broader context of her life. She began to reflect on past experiences and relationships, recognizing how love had shaped her identity and resilience. The support she received during her cancer journey illuminated the importance of cultivating meaningful connections, not just in times of crisis but as a way of life. This realization inspired her to nurture her relationships further, deepening her bonds with those she cherished and fostering new connections based on love and mutual support.

The love that Vanessa experienced during her Radvax therapy inspired her to give back to others facing similar challenges. She became involved in support groups, sharing her story became a way to spread love and hope to others who might be feeling isolated or afraid. She realized that love is a cycle; the more she shared it, the more it multiplied. This newfound purpose enriched her life and provided her with a sense of fulfillment that transcended her struggles.

As her treatment progressed, Vanessa noticed a remarkable shift in her outlook on life. The love she received became a source of strength, enabling her to confront her cancer with a renewed sense of courage. The fear that once consumed her began to dissipate, replaced by a deep appreciation for the moments she shared with loved ones. She learned to embrace life with open arms, understanding that love could be both a shield and a sword in her battle against cancer. It empowered her, reminding her that she had the capacity to face challenges head-on, buoyed by the love that surrounded her.

The culmination of her Radvax therapy marked not just a medical victory but a spiritual awakening. Vanessa emerged from her experience with a profound understanding of the transformative power of love in her life. She began to see her journey with cancer not just as a struggle for survival but as a profound opportunity for growth and connection. The love she received from family, friends, and even strangers had woven itself into the very fabric of her being, shaping her identity and outlook. This newfound perspective filled her with gratitude, as she recognized that love was the thread that tied together her experiences, both joyous and challenging.

In the aftermath of her treatment, Vanessa made a conscious decision to prioritize love in her daily life. She started by expressing her appreciation openly to those who had stood by her side during her cancer journey. Simple gestures, such as handwritten notes, heartfelt conversations, and spontaneous gatherings, became her way of honoring the love that had buoyed her spirits. She found joy in creating moments that allowed her loved ones to feel cherished and valued, understanding that love thrives when it is nurtured and shared.

Moreover, Vanessa's experience inspired her to become more attuned to the world around her. She began to notice the small acts of kindness that often go unnoticed in the hustle and bustle of everyday life. Whether it was a stranger offering a warm smile or someone holding the door open, these simple gestures became reminders of the interconnectedness of humanity. With each encounter, she made it a point to reciprocate that kindness and love, recognizing that every positive interaction contributes to a more compassionate world.

Her journey also ignited a passion for self advocacy, prompting her to raise awareness about the importance of emotional support in cancer treatment. Vanessa began sharing her story and emphasizing how love and community can impact healing. She advocated for integrating emotional and mental health resources into cancer care, believing that patients should receive holistic support that addresses not only their physical health but their emotional well-being as well. Her voice became a beacon for others, encouraging them to seek and offer love in their own journeys.

In her personal relationships, Vanessa discovered a new depth of connection since her diagnosis. She began to engage in deeper conversations with friends and family, discussing not just the surface-level topics but also their fears, dreams, and aspirations. This openness fostered stronger bonds and helped her cultivate a circle of support that was grounded in authenticity. The mutual sharing of vulnerabilities allowed her to witness the healing power of love in real-time, as those around her felt empowered to share their own struggles and triumphs.

As Vanessa continued to embrace love in her life, she also became an advocate for self-care and self-love. She recognized that to give and receive love effectively, she needed to nurture her own well-being. She began to prioritize activities that brought her joy and peace, such as yoga, painting, and spending time in nature. This commitment to self-care not only replenished her energy but also reinforced her belief that love must start from within. The more she cared for herself, the more she could authentically share that love with others.

Vanessa's perspective on challenges also shifted significantly. Rather than viewing obstacles as burdens, she began to see them as opportunities for growth and connection. Each setback became a chance to lean on loved ones for support, reinforcing the idea that love is not just a passive emotion but an active force that can drive resilience. She learned to approach difficulties with a sense of curiosity, asking herself how she could harness the love around her to navigate through tough times.

In reflecting on her journey, Vanessa realized that love is a powerful healer, capable of transcending suffering and fostering hope. It is a force that can unite individuals, creating a tapestry of support that nurtures the spirit. This understanding shaped her daily interactions, prompting her to approach each day with an open heart and a willingness to embrace the love that comes her way. She became a living testament to the idea that love can heal wounds that medicine alone cannot touch.

As she looks to the future, Vanessa remains committed to sharing her journey and the lessons learned about the healing power of love. She dreams of creating a platform where she can connect with others battling cancer, offering support, resources, and a community infused with love. Through this endeavor, she hopes to inspire others to recognize the importance of emotional well-being in their healing journeys. Ultimately, Vanessa's story is one of resilience, transformation, and the undeniable truth that love is the most potent medicine of all.

Chapter Thirty Eight

A Journey of Forgiveness

Vanessa's journey with stage four cancer was not only a battle against the disease but also a profound exploration of forgiveness. From the moment she received her diagnosis, she felt the weight of unresolved emotions and past grievances pressing down on her. The harsh reality of her situation forced her to confront the anger and resentment she had been harboring, pushing her to consider the healing power of forgiveness in her life. What began as a struggle to cope with her illness soon transformed into a transformative journey of self-discovery and emotional release.

At first, the idea of forgiveness felt daunting for Vanessa. She had experienced significant hurt in her life, betrayals from friends, misunderstandings with family, and even her own internal struggles with self-criticism. These emotions bubbled to the surface as she faced the reality of her mortality. Rather than allowing them to consume her, she realized that holding onto these negative feelings was only adding to her pain, both physically and emotionally. This realization marked the beginning of her journey toward forgiveness, a journey she knew would be essential for her healing.

As she delved deeper into her emotions, Vanessa began to explore the roots of her anger. Reflection became a daily practice, where she would journal her thoughts and feelings. She wrote about the people who had hurt her and the situations that had left her feeling betrayed. This act of putting pen to paper served as a cathartic release, allowing her to externalize her pain and begin the process of letting go. She soon discovered that forgiveness was not about condoning the actions of others but about freeing herself from the burden of resentment.

One pivotal moment in Vanessa's journey occurred during a support group session for cancer patients. As she listened to others share their experiences, she was struck by a fellow participant's story of forgiveness. This person spoke about how forgiving those who had hurt them allowed them to find peace amidst their suffering. Inspired by this powerful narrative, Vanessa realized that she, too, could reclaim her power by choosing forgiveness. It was a turning point that ignited a desire within her to explore the possibility of healing through forgiveness.

With this newfound perspective, Vanessa began to reach out to those she felt had wronged her. It was a daunting task, filled with vulnerability and uncertainty. She started with small conversations, expressing her feelings and seeking closure. Some interactions went smoothly, while others were met with resistance or indifference. Yet, with each attempt, she felt a weight lifting from her shoulders. The act of voicing her feelings and seeking understanding became a powerful tool in her journey toward emotional freedom.

Simultaneously, Vanessa realized that self-forgiveness was equally vital. She had often been her harshest critic, replaying moments of perceived failure in her mind. The cancer diagnosis forced her to confront the unrealistic expectations she had set for herself. In recognizing that she was human and deserving of compassion, she began to practice self-acceptance. This shift in mindset allowed her to forgive herself for past mistakes and to embrace her journey without judgment, paving the way for inner peace.

As she continued to navigate this complex emotional landscape, Vanessa found solace in mindfulness practices. Meditation and yoga became essential components of her daily routine, offering her a way to connect with her body and mind. These practices taught her to be present in the moment, allowing her to observe her thoughts and feelings without attachment. Through mindfulness, she learned to acknowledge her anger and sadness without letting them control her. This awareness became a crucial part of her forgiveness journey, as she cultivated a sense of compassion for herself and others.

In her quest for forgiveness, Vanessa also discovered the importance of gratitude. She began to intentionally focus on the positive aspects of her life, even amidst the challenges of cancer. Each day, she would list things she was grateful for, from the support of loved ones to the beauty of nature around her. This practice shifted her perspective, helping her see that while pain and hurt were part of her journey, there was also love and joy to be found. Gratitude became a powerful antidote to resentment, allowing her to reframe her experiences and appreciate the lessons they had taught her.

Through her journey of forgiveness, Vanessa ultimately found a sense of liberation. As she let go of past grievances, she created space for love, compassion, and connection in her life. The relationships that had once felt strained began to heal, and she found herself more open to vulnerability and intimacy. Forgiveness allowed her to cultivate deeper connections with her family and friends, fostering an environment of support that was crucial during her cancer treatment. It was as if the act of forgiving had opened the floodgates to a more profound love and understanding in her life.

As she reflected on her journey, Vanessa realized that forgiveness was not a destination but an ongoing process. She understood that it would take time and effort to fully embrace this new perspective, especially as life continued to present challenges. Yet, with each step she took toward forgiveness, she felt herself growing stronger and more resilient. The emotional weight that had once felt suffocating began to lift, revealing a space filled with hope and possibility. Vanessa recognized that the act of forgiving herself and others was a gift she could give herself, one that would allow her to live more fully in each moment, regardless of the uncertainties surrounding her health. This newfound sense of freedom propelled her forward, motivating her to embrace each day with a renewed sense of purpose.

As Vanessa shared her journey with forgiveness, she realized the impact it had on those around her. Friends and family began to take notice of her transformation. Her vulnerability and honesty about her struggles inspired others to examine their own unresolved feelings and grudges. Conversations shifted from surface-level pleasantries to deeper discussions about forgiveness, healing, and the importance of letting go. It became a collective journey, fostering a sense of community that extended beyond her immediate circle. Vanessa found solace in the idea that her personal journey could also encourage others to embark on their paths toward healing.

In her advocacy work, Vanessa began to incorporate themes of forgiveness into her talks and workshops. She shared her story with cancer patients and survivors, emphasizing how forgiveness could be a powerful tool in managing emotional pain. By creating a safe space for others to discuss their struggles, she helped facilitate conversations about anger, resentment, and the importance of emotional well-being. Vanessa's work resonated deeply with many, as they began to understand that forgiveness is not about absolving others of their actions but about reclaiming one's own power and peace of mind.

One of the most transformative aspects of her journey was the shift in her relationship with her body. Living with stage four cancer had initially filled her with fear and self-doubt. However, as she practiced forgiveness, she began to cultivate a sense of love and appreciation for her body, regardless of its limitations. Vanessa learned to honor her body as it was, celebrating its strength and resilience in the face of adversity. This newfound appreciation fostered a deeper connection between her mind and body, allowing her to approach her treatment with a sense of empowerment rather than defeat.

As Vanessa continued to navigate her health challenges, she understood that forgiveness also meant releasing the need for perfection. There were days when she felt overwhelmed, frustrated, or simply defeated by her illness. Instead of chastising herself for these feelings, she learned to embrace them as part of her journey. This acceptance allowed her to be kinder to herself, recognizing that healing is not a linear process. On days when hope felt distant, she reminded herself that it was okay to feel vulnerable, and that vulnerability was, in itself, a form of strength.

Vanessa's journey also revealed the importance of forgiveness in her relationship with her healthcare team. Initially, she had harbored feelings of frustration toward certain doctors and treatments that hadn't worked as she had hoped. However, as she embraced forgiveness, she realized that her care team was doing their best in an incredibly complex and challenging field. Learning to communicate openly with her doctors about her concerns and feelings allowed her to forge a collaborative relationship built on trust and mutual respect. This shift not only improved her treatment experience but also empowered her to take an active role in her healing process.

In her quieter moments, Vanessa often reflected on the lessons of her journey. She found comfort in the idea that forgiveness is a personal choice, one that can significantly impact one's quality of life. She came to understand that forgiveness is not just about the past; it is a proactive step toward creating a more peaceful future. Each act of forgiveness became an affirmation of her commitment to live authentically and fully, with an open heart ready to embrace both love and challenge.

Through her advocacy and personal journey, Vanessa began to explore the idea of legacy. She wanted her story to serve as a reminder that even in the face of immense pain, one can choose love over resentment. She envisioned creating a foundation aimed at providing resources for cancer patients that emphasized emotional well-being, including workshops on forgiveness, self-acceptance, and resilience. Vanessa hoped to empower others to find their own paths toward healing, demonstrating that love and forgiveness can coexist even amidst the challenges of illness.

As she looked ahead, Vanessa embraced the idea that her journey with cancer was an opportunity for growth, not just for herself but for everyone she encountered. She understood that while her physical health was uncertain, her spirit and heart were vibrant and full of life. Each day, she made a conscious choice to live with intention, extending grace to herself and others. This commitment to forgiveness became a guiding principle, allowing her to navigate the complexities of life with courage, compassion, and a profound sense of hope.

Ultimately, Vanessa recognized that her journey through forgiveness was an ongoing process, one that would continue to evolve as she faced new challenges and experiences. With every step she took, she felt a deeper connection to herself and to others, grounded in love and understanding. Embracing forgiveness became a source of strength that fueled her fight against cancer.

Chapter Thirty Nine

Looking Forward: Beyond Cancer

Vanessa had always been a vibrant soul, known for her infectious laughter and her ability to light up any room she entered. However, the past few years had tested her resilience in ways she could have never imagined. A diagnosis of cancer had thrown her life into disarray, and the once-clear path she envisioned for her future had become shrouded in uncertainty and fear. Yet, as she stood on the precipice of recovery, a newfound sense of hope began to blossom within her, illuminating a future beyond the shadows of her illness.

In the early days of her diagnosis, Vanessa felt engulfed by a storm of emotions, fear, anger, and confusion. The relentless barrage of medical appointments, treatments, and the physical toll of the disease weighed heavily on her. However, as she navigated through the complexities of her treatment, she discovered an inner strength she never knew she possessed. Each challenge she faced became a stepping stone, leading her toward a greater understanding of herself and her life's purpose.

As she completed her treatment, Vanessa found herself reflecting on the experiences that had shaped her journey. She began to see the value in the lessons learned: the importance of resilience, the power of community, and the beauty of vulnerability. Surrounded by family and friends who offered unwavering support, she realized that she was never alone in her fight. This sense of connection fueled her determination to not only survive but to thrive in the aftermath of her battle with cancer.

With each passing day, the fog of uncertainty began to lift, revealing a future filled with possibilities. Vanessa started to envision what lay ahead, considering dreams she had shelved during her illness. She had always wanted to travel, to explore new cultures and meet new people. Now, she found herself daydreaming about distant lands, vibrant marketplaces, and breathtaking landscapes. The world felt like a vast canvas, waiting for her to paint her experiences upon it.

In addition to travel, Vanessa rekindled her passion for writing. Throughout her treatment, she had kept a journal, pouring her thoughts and emotions onto the pages. This practice not only served as a therapeutic outlet but also ignited a desire to share her story with others. She envisioned writing a memoir that would inspire those facing similar challenges, a testament to the resilience of the human spirit. The idea of using her voice to uplift others filled her with excitement and purpose.

Vanessa also began to prioritize her health and well-being in ways she had never considered before. She embraced a holistic approach, incorporating mindfulness practices, healthy eating, and regular exercise into her routine. This newfound dedication to self-care not only strengthened her body but also nurtured her mind and spirit. She realized that taking care of herself was not just a necessity but a celebration of her survival. A way to honor the journey she had endured.

As she looked forward, Vanessa felt a profound sense of gratitude for the life she had lived and the lessons she had learned. She understood that while cancer had changed her, it had also given her a unique perspective on life. She no longer took moments for granted and cherished the simple joys, a sunset, a warm cup of tea, or a heartfelt conversation with a friend. Each day became an opportunity to embrace life fully, to savor experiences that once felt mundane.

Vanessa's relationships also deepened in the wake of her experience. She found herself connecting with others on a more profound level, sharing her story and listening to theirs. She became an advocate for cancer awareness, participating in support groups and community events. By sharing her journey, she discovered the healing power of empathy and connection, realizing that her story could resonate with many others navigating their battles.

As she embraced her new chapter, Vanessa began to set new goals for herself. With an unwavering spirit, she aimed to create a life that reflected her true self. One filled with passion, purpose, and adventure. Whether it was pursuing a new career path, volunteering for causes close to her heart, or simply being present for her loved ones, she felt empowered to take control of her destiny. The future, once a source of anxiety, now beckoned her with open arms.

Vanessa understood that the journey ahead would not be without challenges, but she felt equipped to face them head-on. With an unyielding belief in her strength and the support of her loved ones, she was ready to embrace whatever life had in store. The scars of her past would always remain, but they would serve as reminders of her resilience rather than symbols of defeat.

As she stood on the brink of this new chapter, Vanessa felt a sense of excitement bubbling within her. She was ready to explore the world beyond cancer, to live fully and authentically. With a heart full of hope and a spirit ignited by possibility, she took a deep breath and stepped forward, ready to embrace the adventure that awaited her. The future was hers to shape, and she was determined to make it a beautiful one.

As Vanessa continued her journey into this new chapter of her life, she realized the importance of surrounding herself with positivity and inspiration. She began to curate her environment thoughtfully, filling it with items that uplifted her spirit. Photographs from her travels, quotes from her favorite authors, and mementos from cherished moments. Each piece served as a reminder of her strength, resilience, and the beauty of the world around her. This intentionality in her surroundings allowed her to cultivate an atmosphere of hope and joy, reinforcing her determination to embrace life fully.

One of the first steps Vanessa took toward her dream of traveling was to create a bucket list of destinations she had always wanted to explore. From the vibrant streets of places she's never seen, to the serene beaches of Florida each location represented not just a place to visit, but a chance to experience life in a new and transformative way. She found herself intrigued by cultures, cuisines, and languages, her excitement growing with each new discovery. The anticipation of future adventures filled her with a sense of purpose, motivating her to work towards her goals with renewed vigor.

In her quest for personal growth, Vanessa also sought out opportunities to learn. She enrolled in workshops and online courses that piqued her interest, from creative writing to photography. Engaging with new concepts and skills reignited her passion for learning, allowing her to express herself and explore her creativity. Each class became a stepping stone on her path of self-discovery, unveiling layers of her identity she hadn't fully understood before. This commitment to continuous learning became a source of joy, fueling her confidence and reaffirming her belief in her ability to adapt and thrive.

As Vanessa explored her newfound passion for journaling, she began to share her story through blogging. She created a platform where she could articulate her experiences and feelings, providing insight into her journey with cancer and recovery. This outlet not only allowed her to process her emotions but also connected her with others who found solace in her words. The feedback she received was heartwarming; readers expressed how her honesty inspired them in their own struggles, creating a sense of community that enriched her life even further.

In the midst of her journaling journey, Vanessa met others who inspired her with their own stories of resilience. Through online forums and journaling groups, she connected with individuals from various walks of life, each sharing their unique narratives. These connections forged friendships that transcended the boundaries of illness. Together, they celebrated each other's victories, whether big or small, and leaned on one another during tough times. This network of understanding and encouragement became a vital part of her life, reminding her that she was never alone on her journey.

As the seasons changed, so did Vanessa's perspective on life. She began to embrace the beauty of impermanence, recognizing that each moment was a gift. With this newfound appreciation, she made a conscious effort to practice gratitude daily. She started a gratitude journal where she documented the little things that brought her joy. The warmth of the sun on her skin, the laughter shared with friends, or the simple act of enjoying a quiet moment with a cup of tea. This practice transformed her outlook, allowing her to focus on the present rather than worrying about what the future might hold.

Feeling inspired by her journey, Vanessa decided to get involved in initiatives focused on wellness and mental health. She wrote articles pthat aimed to help others navigate their own challenges, sharing her insights on mindfulness and self-care. Engaging with others in these settings brought her immense joy, as she witnessed the power of connection and support. Each interaction reinforced her belief in the importance of community and the healing that could come from shared experiences.

As she immersed herself in these initiatives, Vanessa found herself drawn to the world of holistic healing. She began exploring practices such as yoga, meditation, and nutrition, discovering how they could enhance her overall well-being. Each new practice became a tool for self-discovery, helping her cultivate a deeper understanding of her body and mind. This journey into holistic health not only enriched her life but also empowered her to take charge of her health in ways she had never imagined before.

With her heart open and her spirit renewed, Vanessa was excited to take up painting as a form of self-expression. The act of painting became a therapeutic escape, allowing her to express emotions she often found difficult to articulate. The vibrant colors and fluid brushstrokes reflected her inner journey, capturing both her struggles and triumphs. Through her art, she discovered a new form of communication, one that resonated deeply with her soul.

As Vanessa looked ahead, she understood that her journey of healing and self-discovery was an ongoing process. She was committed to continuously evolving and exploring new facets of herself. The scars of her past would always remain, but they would serve as reminders of her resilience rather than symbols of defeat. Embracing life with open arms, she felt a sense of excitement bubbling within her, ready to explore the world beyond.

Chapter Forty

A Legacy of Hope and Healing

Although Vanessa's journey with kidney cancer began unexpectedly, altering the course of her life in unimaginable ways. What initially felt like a devastating blow transformed into a powerful narrative of resilience, hope, and healing. Vanessa's experience became a beacon of light for others navigating the tumultuous waters of cancer, demonstrating the profound impact of determination and community support.

As Vanessa faced her diagnosis, she realized the importance of understanding her illness. Armed with an unwavering spirit, she immersed herself in research, exploring every aspect of kidney cancer. She learned about treatment options, the latest advancements in research, and the necessity of advocating for her own health. This knowledge equipped her with the tools to make informed decisions about her care, allowing her to actively participate in her healing journey rather than merely being a passive recipient of treatment.

Throughout the grueling process of surgery and recovery, Vanessa discovered the power of Family and community. She connected with other survivors and patients through support groups, where shared experiences provided solace and strength. These interactions fostered a sense of belonging, reminding her that she was not alone in her battle. The stories of hope and survival from fellow cancer warriors inspired Vanessa to maintain a positive outlook, even on days when the weight of her diagnosis felt overwhelming.

Vanessa's resilience was further tested during her treatment regimen, which included targeted therapies and immunotherapy. The side effects were challenging, often leaving her fatigued and vulnerable. However, she approached each day with a renewed sense of purpose, focusing on self-care and wellness practices. Yoga, meditation, and journaling became essential components of her routine, enabling her to cultivate mindfulness and emotional balance amidst the chaos of her diagnosis and treatment.

The turning point in Vanessa's journey came when she decided to share her story publicly. Inspired by her own experiences, she began journaling, detailing her ups and downs, the lessons learned, and the triumphs celebrated. Her candid reflections resonated with many, touching hearts and igniting hope in those facing similar struggles. Vanessa's words became a source of inspiration, encouraging others to embrace their stories and seek healing through vulnerability and connection.

In her Self advocacy efforts, Vanessa sought to raise awareness about kidney cancer, emphasizing the need for early detection and research funding. She partnered with local organizations to organize community events and educational seminars aimed at spreading knowledge about the disease. Through her tireless efforts, Vanessa not only empowered others but also fostered a sense of urgency around the importance of proactive health measures, reinforcing the belief that education can save lives.

As Vanessa emerged from her treatment journey, she began to reflect on the profound lessons learned during her battle with cancer. Gratitude became a central theme in her life; she cherished the little moments that often went unnoticed before her diagnosis. This newfound perspective encouraged her to prioritize relationships and experiences that brought joy and fulfillment, shaping her into a more compassionate and empathetic individual.

Vanessa's legacy of hope and healing extended beyond her own recovery. Inspired by the support she received during her journey, she launched a non-profit organization dedicated to supporting kidney cancer patients and their families. The organization provided resources, emotional support, and financial assistance to those facing similar challenges, ensuring that no one had to navigate their journey alone. Vanessa's commitment to giving back created a ripple effect of healing within her community.

Her self advocacy work also included collaborating with healthcare professionals to improve patient care and access to treatment. Vanessa understood the complexities of the healthcare system and fought tirelessly for policies that would enhance the quality of life for cancer patients. She became a voice for the voiceless, emphasizing the importance of compassionate care and the need for systemic changes that prioritize patient well-being.

As Vanessa continues her journey as a survivor, she embodies the essence of hope and resilience. Her story serves as a reminder that life can be redefined even in the face of adversity. Through her unwavering spirit, advocacy, and dedication to helping others, Vanessa has created a legacy that transcends her personal experience with kidney cancer. Her commitment to hope and healing inspires countless individuals, reminding them that they too can rise above their challenges and emerge stronger.

In a world where cancer can feel isolating and daunting, Vanessa's legacy stands as a testament to the strength of the human spirit. She has transformed her battle into a mission of hope, healing, and empowerment for others. As she looks to the future, Vanessa remains committed to spreading awareness, supporting others, and living life to the fullest, ensuring that her legacy will continue to shine brightly for generations to come.

As Vanessa reflected on her journey, she understood that her experience with kidney cancer had irrevocably shaped her identity and purpose. Each challenge she faced had not only tested her resilience but had also illuminated the paths that lay ahead. With every setback, she had discovered strengths she never knew she possessed. Vanessa realized that her story was not just about surviving cancer; it was about thriving in its aftermath and using her experiences to inspire hope in others.

With a dedicated team of supporters, friends, and family. Vanessa felt a deep sense of fulfillment as she witnessed the impact of her self advocacy work. Vanessa who once felt isolated found solace and strength in her friends and family. Each trial overcome reinforced her belief in the importance of shared experiences and collective healing. She knew that her words had the power to resonate with others, to ignite hope, and to encourage those facing their battles. Vanessa's authenticity and vulnerability struck a chord, fostering connections with people from all walks of life.

In her personal life, Vanessa cherished every moment, embracing spontaneity and adventure. She traveled to places she had only dreamed of visiting, each destination symbolizing the freedom of living life fully. From relaxing on sun-soaked beaches, each experience served as a reminder of her victory over fear. Vanessa learned to appreciate the beauty in the everyday, finding joy in the simple pleasures that life had to offer.

Through her travels, Vanessa also sought to connect with other cancer survivors around the world. She initiated a project that invited survivors to share their stories, creating a global tapestry of resilience and hope. Each story highlighted the unique human experience of battling cancer, showcasing the various ways in which individuals found strength and healing. Vanessa compiled these narratives into her journal.

Every word, marked a significant milestone in Vanessa's journey. She loved, engaging with readers and survivors across the country. The words within her journal sparked conversations about cancer, survival, and the importance of community support. Vanessa understood that sharing these narratives was a powerful way to foster understanding and empathy, bridging the gap between those who had experienced cancer and those who had not.

As Vanessa's self advocacy grew, she also invested time in her personal growth. She enrolled in courses on psychology and holistic health, determined to deepen her understanding of healing. This knowledge not only enriched her own life but also enhanced her ability to support others. Vanessa began to incorporate holistic practices into her life, providing resources that emphasized mental and emotional well-being alongside traditional medical care.

With the support of her growing kinship, Vanessa's articles on wellness tailored for cancer patients and survivors, on mindfulness, nutrition, and emotional resilience, empowering others to take an active role in their healing journeys. Vanessa's commitment to holistic care resonated deeply, as many others expressed gratitude for the chance to explore new avenues of wellness and self-care.

As she navigated the complexities of life after cancer, Vanessa also became a self advocate for policy changes that would improve access to care and support for cancer patients. She collaborated with healthcare professionals and lawmakers, sharing her story to illustrate the urgent need for comprehensive support systems. Vanessa understood the significance of fighting for systemic change, ensuring that future generations of patients would have better access to resources and support.

In moments of quiet reflection, Vanessa often revisited the lessons learned throughout her journey. She recognized that hope is not merely a feeling but a choice. One that can be cultivated even in the darkest of times. Her journey had taught her that healing is a multifaceted process, encompassing the physical, emotional, and social aspects of life. It is a continual evolution, one that she would embrace with open arms.

As Vanessa looked to the future, she felt a profound sense of purpose. Her legacy of hope and healing extended far beyond her own experience; it was woven into the fabric of her community and the lives she touched. Vanessa knew that while her battle with kidney cancer had shaped her, it was her response to that challenge that defined her. With a heart full of gratitude and a spirit of determination, she embraced the road ahead, ready to inspire others to find their own light in the face of adversity.

As the final chapter of her journal drew to a close, Vanessa penned a heartfelt message to her readers. "In every struggle, there exists the seed of hope," she wrote. "Together, we can nurture that hope, allowing it to blossom.

Don't miss out!

Visit the website below and you can sign up to receive emails whenever Amanda Ventura publishes a new book. There's no charge and no obligation.

https://books2read.com/r/B-A-AQBIC-DSCBF

BOOKS 2 READ

Connecting independent readers to independent writers.

About the Author

Amanda Ventura, a linguist originally from Texas, has a strong enthusiasm for languages, writing, and culture. Her unique personal experiences have the potential to resonate deeply with many, and she aims to share her story to inspire and connect with a global audience. Amanda Ventura aims to make a positive societal impact by sharing her experiences.

Read more at https://www.amazon.com/author/venturaamanda.

www.ingramcontent.com/pod-product-compliance
Lightning Source LLC
LaVergne TN
LVHW082247150826
845677LV00009B/1552

* 9 7 9 8 2 2 4 7 8 0 3 4 1 *